Born David Tynan-O'Mahony in the Dublin countryside in 1936, Dave Allen enjoyed a career that spanned
over 40 years. His sharp-eyed observation of the everyday and his elegance and ease in the telling changed the
face of stand-up comedy. His television work included
ground-breaking shows such as *Tonight with Dave Allen*
in Australia, the award-winning *Dave Allen at Large* for
the BBC, the Carlton series *Dave Allen*, a television play
by Alan Bennett called *One Fine Day* and numerous
documentaries. From Australia to Zambia his shows
were sold worldwide.

His sell-out one-man stage shows included West End
runs at the Vaudeville, Haymarket, Albery and Strand
Theatres, many tours of the UK, Australia, Canada and
New Zealand as well as shows in America and Hong
Kong. He appeared on stage in other guises too: enjoying two Edna O'Brien plays and playing in Peter Pan
opposite Maggie Smith at London's Coliseum.

In 1996 Dave Allen received a Lifetime Achievement
Award at the Comedy Awards.

He told his life through stories while holding a mirror
up to ours. He loved wildflowers, the Irish rugby team,
art, whisky, laughter, the company of friends, peace of
mind, and his family.

Dave Allen died on 10 March 2006.

The Essential Dave Allen

Edited by Graham McCann
With a Foreword by Sir Bill Cotton, CBE

HODDER

Copyright © Dave Allen
Illustrations within the text © Dave Allen
Introductions © Graham McCann 2005
Foreword © Sir Bill Cotton, CBE 2005

First published in Great Britain in 2005 by Hodder and Stoughton
A division of Hodder Headline

A Hodder Paperback

5

A CIP catalogue record for this title is available from the British Library

ISBN 978 0 340 89945-8

Typeset in Minion by Servis Filmsetting Ltd, Manchester

Printed and bound in the UK by
CPI Mackays, Chatham ME5 8TD

Hodder Headline's policy is to use papers that are natural, renewable and recyclable
products and made from wood grown in sustainable forests. The logging and
manufacturing processes are expected to conform to the environmental regulations of
the country of origin.

Hodder and Stoughton Ltd
A division of Hodder Headline
338 Euston Road
London NW1 3BH

For Cullen, Albert and Emma

Contents

Illustrations

~

1. A portrait of the artist as a young man, circa 1957.

2. The Tynan-O'Mahony brothers – Peter, David and John – out with their dogs in County Dublin.

3. The career begins at Butlin's: 'At first, I hated going on stage, but after a time wild horses wouldn't drag me off. I was getting my first real taste of show-business, and I loved it'.

4. Peter Tynan-O'Mahony photographed his television set as his brother, Dave, made his television debut on the BBC show *New Faces*: 'The longest, most terrifying three minutes of my life'.

4.b Appearing as MC of television's *Sunday Night at the London Palladium* in the mid-Sixties: 'Dave's doing a great job for us,' said ATV boss Lew Grade. 'He's in the star bracket as a TV host'.

5. On *The Val Doonican Show* in 1965: 'He was really a lovely artist to watch,' Doonican recalled. 'I admired the way he told a story, his impeccable timing and the material was funny'.

6. Sketches from *Dave Allen At Large*: 'I hope that God has a sense of humour . . .'

7. With three of his 'wonderful repertory company': Jacqueline Clarke, Michael Sharvell-Martin and Ronnie Brody.

8. This handsome man: the sit-down stand-up in action on his own prime-time show.

*

9. Relaxing with the writer Alan Bennett during the making of the TV play *One Fine Day* (1979).

10. *The Royal Gala Television Performance*, BBC TV Centre, 1970 (*left to right*: the cast of *Dad's Army*, Queen Elizabeth II, Dudley Moore, Huw Wheldon, Dave Allen, Eddie Braben, Ernie Wise, Eric Morecambe and Vera Lynn).

10. In his dressing room before one of his hugely successful stage shows in the 1980s.

11. 'In case you wonder what I do, I tend to stroll around and chat,' Dave Allen used to tell his audience. 'I'd be grateful if you'd refrain from doing the same'.

12. The masterful comic in action, making people think as well as laugh: 'Why – "why" is a wonderful word'.

13. 'I don't ridicule religion. I ridicule some concepts of what people believe religion is. I firmly believe that if anybody wants to do anything in their life, they have the right to do it'.

14. Launching the suspense collection he edited, *A Little Night Reading*, in 1974: 'It is not so much that I believe in

the supernatural,' he said of his interest in such fiction, 'but like many people I have a fear of the tricks my imagination might play on me'.

15. Samuel L Jackson considered him 'cool,' and Robert Stephens declared that he could have been a movie star: Dave Allen was the comic with leading-man looks.

16. From controversial clocks to turkey pluckers: Dave Allen photographed by his great friend, Nobby Clark, in London in 1994.

Picture Acknowledgements
All illustrations within the text © Dave Allen.
© BBC Photo Library: 5, 6, 7, 8, 10 top. © Nobby Clark: Endpapers, 10 bottom, 11, 12, 15, 16. © Courtesy Granada: 9. © Bill Mitchell: 13. © Private Collection: 1, 2, 3 top. © John Silvester: 14. © Peter Tynan-O'Mahony: 3 bottom, 4.

Acknowledgements

I would like to thank Nick Davies for all of his encouragement throughout this project. My grateful thanks also go to Sir Bill Cotton, Vivienne Clore, Michael Sharvell-Martin, Jacqui Clarke, Peter Vincent, John Ammonds, Hugh Stuckey, Els Boonen, Gavin Barker, Steve Dobell, Ian Fraser, Dick Geary, Mic Cheetham and Silvana Dean, as well as to my mother and my late father.

The following institutions and organisations have all assisted me in one way or another: the BBC Film and TV Library; the BBC Written Archives Centre; BBC Worldwide; the BFI; the University of Cambridge Library; the British Newspaper Library; the National Film and Sound Archive of Australia; ScreenSound Australia; The Richard Stone Partnership; and the *Guardian*; the *Irish Times*; the *Age*; and the *New York Times*.

This book would not have been completed without the consent, kindness and advice of Dave Allen's family. It was a privilege to work with them. What follows from me is for Jane and Ed and Karin and Cullen.

Graham McCann, Cambridge, August 2005

Foreword

I first met Dave Allen when I was looking for someone to do five minutes a week in a new BBC series with Val Doonicàn. Richard Stone, Dave's agent, took me to a roadhouse on the Maidstone bypass where Dave was appearing, having recently left Australia under a cloud.

As I remember there were about a dozen or so people scattered around a very dark room, all seemingly intent on getting their partners on to the dance floor, only reacting favourably to Dave's shaggy dog story about Noah and his sons clearing all the animal droppings from the ark. The punchline was that it took two days to heave the stuff over the side, and in 1492, Christopher Columbus discovered it.

I thought he was terrific and got my boss, Tom Sloan, to go and see him at the Cabaret Club the following week. Tom, a military looking man, appeared very like the type that frequented the club. He arrived whilst Dave was having a drink at the bar and greeted him with, "There you are, I've been looking for you everywhere." Dave immediately thought Tom was trying to pick him up, excused himself and moved away with Tom in hot pursuit. The chase only stopped when I arrived and introduced them.

It was some time later when Dave had done the

Doonican show and a series on ITV that we did *Dave Allen At Large*, a sketch show with stand-up – or in this case "sit down" – with Dave holding, unbelievably now, a glass of amber fluid and a cigarette. The series was a great success and we started discussing a further series for the following year. Dave told me he was working out of town and asked if I could visit him the following week to continue discussions. I agreed and as I left he said, "By the way, I'm working in the Mandarin Hotel in Hong Kong next week. Don't forget you said you'd come."

My few days in Hong Kong with Dave Allen were an education. He insisted I stayed in his suite and I learned how to be a gentleman's gentleman, answering the phone and serving the drinks at Dave's happy hour.

He lived the other way round in Hong Kong. Breakfast at four, happy hour from six to seven, followed by light lunch at nine, show at ten-thirty, then out on the town, including a massive Chinese meal at about three a.m., bed at God knows what time – it nearly killed me. During his happy hour we often had the management and fellow travellers over for a drink. The PR lady was particularly good-looking and I engaged her in conversation. Dave immediately offered to take a picture of us on the balcony using my camera. He insisted on posing us in a fond embrace, and I was looking forward to having this souvenir from my stay. When I got it developed, like many unsuspecting tourists around the world who had gratefully let Dave take a picture of them, I had a photograph of two pairs of feet.

I fell for every ruse he played. The times I said, "I think

you've got the wrong number," to a Chinese madman trying to say he was delivering my order or to the local park keeper complaining that our dog had crapped on the flowers, were legion.

Being responsible for Dave's BBC Television shows was not all beer and skittles. There was the matter of the Lord Provost who insisted on an official meeting with the Director General to complain that the BBC had given free rein to Dave Allen to destroy the Catholic Church. Alasdair Milne and myself were bidden to attend the meeting. Dave was not. The Lord Provost was paraplegic with a minder who made Martin Johnson look like a dwarf and who carried him to his chair. To say the Provost was a committed Roman Catholic would only be half the story. What he didn't know was that the Director General, Charles Curran, was a serious practising, if not perfect, Roman Catholic himself.

The meeting started with a discussion about which Catholic journal they read, the *Tablet* or the *Herald*. There was no agreement even on that, and after ten gruelling rounds in which Alasdair and I took no part at all, the Director General landed a decisive blow, stating that he could not accept that the Catholic Church could not, or would not, survive the wit of Dave Allen, whose shows he personally enjoyed immensely.

My reporting of this meeting had a downside. From then on, whenever I exercised any type of editorial control over Dave's shows, usually on the matter of language, his reply was that he'd go and see his friend the Director General.

Dave's place in comedy was in the transition from music hall and variety stand-up comedians to the more intimate comedy on television. In fact he was a leading exponent of it. Dave was confident and comfortable with the audience. He had the best of all worlds because he knew what he wanted to do and was able to arrange it. A West End season of his one-man show and later a tour of the major cities, then a TV series, would take up a period of three years, during which he continually sought out and collected new material.

He was a very private person – not aggressively so, but socially he would observe rather than dominate. He was the main proponent of the laid-back type of comedy on often serious subjects. Many have affected and copied it, but Dave was the real thing.

Farewell, our friend. I've got a funny feeling we will meet again, and if it's in the kingdom of heaven, God help us both.

Bill Cotton, Swanage, August 2005

Introduction

*Comedy is knowing how vulnerable you are; how
silly and how trite and how petty and how wonderful
and all those things that make a human being.*

∼

The spotlight picked him out: the cool, calm, darkly
handsome man sitting up smart and straight in his black
leather chair, with half a Gauloise between his fingers, a
glass of the good stuff by his side and more than an
evening's worth of mischief sparkling inside his eyes. He
welcomed you in, and then started sharing stories –
some of them short, many of them tall and one or two
of them strange – that made you laugh and made you
think and made you want him to stay a while longer and
share a few more. He was Dave Allen, the smooth, suave
sit-down stand-up comic, and this collection is a cele-
bration of his very special craft.

It was his craft that he wanted commemorated (he was
content to keep the rest of his life private, and thus remain

one of our best-known unknowns). It was through his craft, through that wonderfully precise yet playful way that he had with words, that he connected so well with his audience. Each time a story elicited the happy effect, he used to give the ends of his waistcoat a quick little tug, brush away a stray bit of invisible lint from the top of his knees or the front of his lap, and then smile the most satisfied of smiles: the bond between him and his audience was growing stronger and stronger and stronger.

It was not just how he delivered his humour, however; it was also what that humour was about. Dave Allen made an authentic connection with our everyday lives. He seemed to care about what we cared about, get irritated and exasperated by the same sorts of big and trivial things, and rage as much as we did at a world full of wild and witless contradictions.

He helped to keep you sane: no matter how many people appeared ready to treat the illogical as logical and the patently unjust as perfectly fair, you knew that you could always rely on Dave Allen to respond in a reassuringly rational and rigorous manner. He always seemed real. He always seemed like one of us.

Dave Allen was a comedian for the duration. He was there for all of the rites of passage, and all of the hopes and fears and dreams and doubts that shaped and shook our lives. He never outgrew you, nor did you ever outgrow him: he always had something to say that engaged and moved and amused you, whether you were young, middle-aged or mature; religious, agnostic or atheistic; conservative, liberal or socialist; safely settled, occasionally insecure or chronically bemused and bewildered. Once he had made you laugh once or twice, you somehow knew that he would go on making you laugh for the rest of your life. He was that kind of comedian. He was bright enough, honest enough and incisive enough to be as rare and as special as that.

How did he get to be that good? Some of the seeds were certainly sown during his earliest years in Ireland. The youngest of three sons (the other two being Peter and John), he was born David Tynan-O'Mahony at Templeogue in County Dublin on 6 July 1936, and grew up surrounded by seasoned storytellers and well-read relations. His English mother, Jean, was a woman who revered her adopted literary tradition, while his Irish father, Gerard John Cullen (the general manager of the *Irish Times*), was a drinking partner of the author Brian O'Nolan (who also wrote under the two celebrated pseudonyms of Flann O'Brien and Myles na Gopaleen[1]) and was a warm, witty, larger-than-life character known to colleagues as 'Cullie the Clown Prince of Irish journalism';[2] his paternal grandmother, Nora, had been features editor of the *Freeman's Journal* (a publication that could boast W.B. Yeats among its contributors); one of Cullie's cousins, Eoin O'Mahony (known affectionately to all as 'The Pope') was a mellow-tongued barrister, 'wandering scholar' and well-seasoned raconteur whose stories made him welcome at all of Dublin's best dinner tables; and one of his aunts, Katherine ('KT') Tynan, was a noted poet and novelist and a leading figure in the Celtic literary revival.[3]

It was his father, especially, who, with his natural flair for the narrative combined with his considerable skills as a mimic, showed him just how magical and memorable a well-told tale could be: 'Sometimes in the evenings [my father] gathered my brothers and me around the hearth to tell us a story before we went to bed. They were frequently true, and often associated with Irish history, but there was always a special air of apprehension and excitement when he related one of his suspense stories, of which he had an endless collection.'[4] Some of these stories (such as 'The Monkey's Paw' by W.W. Jacobs, 'The Black Cat' by Edgar Allan Poe and 'The Inn of Two Witches' by Joseph Conrad) would end up being re-published in a collection, called *A Little Night Reading*, that the adult Dave Allen compiled, but many more of them, recalled with much the same timing and tone as his father, would inspire those moments during the television show when the lights went down, the audience fell silent and the comedy turned dark until the scares led back to the laughs.

There were other early influences outside of the extended Tynan-O'Mahony family, including a white-haired and white-bearded local individual by the name of Old Malachi Horn – whose finely-spun fictions soon found an avid fan in young David. 'I used to play truant from school just to go for a ride in his pony and trap, and listen to legends of wild banshees and headless coachmen.'[5] Silver-tongued old lollygaggers like Horn showed the boy how to construct clever little things with words – vivid verbal pictures, elaborate mental puzzles and charmingly dramatised dialogues – that tapped into a deep and rich Celtic tradition: 'We are a talking nation,' Dave Allen would reflect, acknowledging his debt to all of those peripatetic storytellers who showed him subtle ways to 'make things interesting'.[6]

David and his two brothers also used to sit at the feet, each New Year's Eve, of the many representatives of literary Dublin's great and good (such as the poet Austin Clarke, Brian O'Nolan and the poet and theatre director F.R. Higgins) who used to gather together at 'Cherryfield' in Templeogue to share a drink, compare shaggy dog stories and celebrate the imminent birthday of their old friend Cullie Tynan-O'Mahony: 'My father was born on New Year's Day in 1900,' the adult Dave Allen would explain. 'He was the first baby born in Ireland in the new century. And, consequently, there was a fairly good shindig every New Year's Eve.'[7] In the presence of those kinds of cultured guests, the Tynan-O'Mahony brothers heard the English language being elevated to the most sumptuous and dextrous of levels, and recognised the precision with which every word was plucked and placed.

There were negative influences, too, in the form of all the various cold-eyed theological pedagogues who managed to make every parable sound achingly plain and painfully predictable. Being educated (in 'Latin grammar, guilt and mathematics') by the Loreto nuns (whom he later dubbed 'the Gestapo in drag'), the little Sisters of Mercy ('or Sisters of Little Mercy'[8]), the Holy Ghost Fathers and the Carmelite priests ('God's storm troopers') served to make the adolescent David acutely averse to any world that thought it could do without the slightest sliver of doubt. 'I detested them so much,' he said of these stern and sometimes brutal dogmatists. 'They interfered greatly with my freedom, they interfered with my physicality – they hit me, they pulled my hair, they punched me, they demeaned me – and now, when I think about it, I'm quite angry, because none of them were qualified teachers. These were members of a religious order who were then made teachers, but none of them had been *trained* as teachers. They beat you, that's what they did. I mean, if you didn't learn Latin, they'd still get it into you somehow.'[9]

David Tynan-O'Mahony grew up, therefore, as an imaginative, observant, slyly irreverent and relatively eloquent young man – a bit of a gadfly with the gift of the gab – who was happy to embrace, rather than hide from, all of the ironies in life, calling himself an atheist but then adding, 'Thank God!'. 'I really do believe,' he later said, 'that humour is not so much about laughing at other people as at what you do yourself and how you react.'[10]

His nascent wit seemed destined to flourish within the genre of journalism, because, upon leaving school at the age of sixteen, he followed in the footsteps of his late father (who had died prematurely, when David was only twelve, in 1948) and joined a newspaper, the *Irish Independent*, as a front office clerk. 'Then I got a job as a cub reporter on the the *Drogheda Times*,' he later recalled, 'but I was pretty bad at that and I ended up in London looking for a Fleet Street job which I totally failed to find.'[11] His next move (in the summer of 1955) took him away from the business of print and into the world of performance: he became, of all things, a Butlin's Redcoat at a holiday camp in Skegness.

It was quite a bold departure for someone who had only performed in front of the public once before – fifteen years ago in a convent – and his contribution on that occasion had earned him nothing more than a slap:

That was when I was at the Loreto nuns, when I was really very small. They were putting on a play and there were three parts in it: the butcher, the baker, the candlestick maker. And I was chosen as the candlestick maker. And then I lost the part – the part was taken away from me because the nuns said I didn't have enough discipline. I was four years of age! So they gave me a job as a frog. The wicked witch was turned into a frog at the end of the play. I had this little froggy costume, and I could wear my vest and underpants. But by the time that we did the play, I'd grown a bit, so I couldn't get into the costume with my vest and my underpants on, so I had to strip off to get into this thing. And then there was a puff of smoke, the witch disappeared and I bounded on as the frog – and got a great big laugh. And I was bouncing around – and I was only supposed to go round once and then come off, but now people were laughing and I was enjoying it, it was great – so I was bounding and bounding, and I didn't know that what had actually happened was that the zip had opened. So I was exposing myself. And

I wasn't getting laughs – I was getting laughs because my *dick* was showing![12]

At Butlin's, however, he knew exactly what he was doing, and what he was doing there prompted a positive response:

You were called a 'Camp Host'. You were there basically to make it easy for the campers – to show them around, make sure that they enjoyed themselves. And then the Redcoats used to put on a show themselves – a kind of revue type of thing. And I got into that, and there were a couple of sketches and I played in the sketches. A piece of scenery broke one time, and I had to go out front, and while I was standing out there I thought, 'Well, I may as well tell a couple of gags,' so I did, got a giggle, and then somebody said, 'You should extend that a little bit more.' Then they gave me a five or six minute spot on the Redcoat show and that was really where it started to develop.[13]

He formed a double-act with his fellow Redcoat Al Page for a second Butlin's season – this time at Filey in Yorkshire – and then coped with the camps on his own in Clacton, Saltdene, Margate and then Skegness once again before heading back to London and braving the toughest club circuit of the time:

The first professional date I did was in a place called Collins Music Hall in Islington. That was my first date. And it was a strip house. The nudes couldn't move at the time. There'd just be tableaux. They'd be Joan of Arc, or Helen of Troy, or something like that. The tabs would open and I would say, 'And here is Helen of Troy before Paris comes to take her,' the curtains would open and this woman would be standing there totally still. And they were always trying to break the rules. So somebody said: 'What if we got a bit of chiffon, and draped it all around her, and then got a fan on the side of the stage and blow, so *she* doesn't move but there's a certain amount of movement *to* her. . . ?' So they went off and they got an industrial fan, about eight feet in circumference, and they turned this thing on and it went: WHOOOOOSH! Now, she had – I mean, I've never seen anything like it before or since – but she had the *longest* pubic hair in the world! She'd stand there, in this breeze, and her pubic hair was going [*mimes a long trail of hair flapping away right through her legs and far behind her*]. Now, we did no business throughout the week – nude shows would have forty followers in rain coats and that was it – but within half an hour [of this hair thing happening] the theatre was full. This was the talk of the town – pubic hair that can blow two feet from behind your bum![14]

It was here, walking on and off to the sound of his own footsteps while the men in the macs waited impatiently for their next glimpse of breast, bottom and trailing hair, that David Tynan-O'Mahony learned how to adapt his storytelling technique for the stage, keep his nerve in the face of indifference or downright hostility and inject a little more aggression, a little bit more of an edge, into his smooth and fluid delivery.

He worked hard, kept learning and, slowly but surely, he built up a fair-sized local following – and even managed to make his first fleeting television appearance, on a BBC talent show called *New Faces*, in 1959. It was, he would recall, 'the longest, most terrifying three minutes of my life'.[15] Some of London's movers and shakers took notice, and he was signed up in 1960 by an eminent theatrical agent, Richard Stone, who liked his act but reasoned that, to improve his chances of establishing himself in England, he would have to change his name. According to Stone, not enough English people would know how to pronounce O'Mahony. The comedian soon came to the same conclusion:

I tried 'Dave O'Mahony', and I'd arrive at places and it would be [spelt on the playbills] 'Dave O'Mally' or 'Dave Maloney' or 'O'Maloney'. So I thought, well, 'Tynan' is simple enough, so I tried 'Tynan', but 'Tynan', for whatever reason, became 'Tyrone' and 'Tannen' and 'Tinnen', and so I never knew who the bloody hell I was! By then I had an agent, Richard Stone, and I was sitting looking at his list of clients, and there was nobody with an 'A', so I thought, well, if I had a surname beginning with 'A' I'd be top of the list. So I changed my name to Allen.[16]

The newly-named Dave Allen spent the next couple of years broadening his experience in Britain, playing to audiences encompassing a wider range of ages, backgrounds and tastes. He entertained the families at the seaside resorts, the young adults in the metropolitan nightclubs and the many raucous teenagers who gathered in the run-down provincial cinemas that now served as places for youth-oriented Variety, rock and pop. He also appeared in 1962 as the resident comic and MC on the same bill that boasted The Beatles, and then joined the legendary jazz singer Sophie Tucker (the so-called 'last of the red-hot mommas') for a short tour of South Africa. Then, in 1963, he began an eight-week trip to Australia that would turn into a hugely successful two-year stay.

Apprehensive though he was when he first stepped on Australian soil, Dave Allen soon came to feel that he had probably arrived in the right place at the right time:

The first date I ever worked in Australia was Kogarah Working Men's Club, or whatever it was called – the RSL [the Returned Servicemen's Club]. And I couldn't believe it, because I arrived on Easter Sunday and thought, 'Where have I arrived?' Because I've arrived in Sydney and there are people playing pitch and toss all over the place; I mean, the whole city is just gambling – at the airport, driving in, there're all great groups of people throwing money down. I thought, 'What sort of place is this?' I didn't know that it was just the one day that it was legalised! And that night I worked in Kogarah at the Returned Servicemen's Club, and as I was standing at the side of the stage the place just went dark, and a man with a bugle played the Last Post, and everybody said the Lord's Prayer! I didn't know what the hell this was about. I mean, I really didn't. I thought: 'What am I *doing* here? Why are they all *praying*?' And then the next thing was: a girl runs on, and the lights go up, and she starts to take her clothes off! So I thought: 'Well, it's a great society! Everything's going for them now – they've got prayers, sin, drink and the lot!'[17]

Australia, in turn, wasted no time at all in taking to Dave Allen. Booked by the producer Frank Sheldon to publicise his tour on GTV Channel 9's *In Melbourne Tonight*, he made such a positive impression on the local viewing public that bags of fan mail, addressed simply to 'Dave Allen', began arriving at the station within a couple of days of his brief appearance.

By the time that his tour was coming close to its conclusion, he was offered a television show all of his own in Sydney on Channel 9:

They wanted to do a *Tonight* type of chat show, like Jack Paar's in America, so they gave me a pilot, and it took off. It was ninety minutes, live, with an open end – which meant that if it was going well at the end of ninety minutes they didn't chop into it; you'd just finish ten or fifteen minutes late. It was great, because it was live and you had to *learn*, because the camera didn't lie: you were there, you were on, and if you fell over you fell over.[18]

The pilot led to a series, *Tonight with Dave Allen*, which grew into one of the most successful programmes in the history of Australian television. It provided Dave Allen with a context that, in terms of the development of his television technique, was inspirational. He eschewed the usual reliance on tame and laboured celebrity plugs, seized on every opportunity to feature unknown and unusual people (such as the man who electrocuted his fruit trees in the hope of promoting their growth, and the reformed alcoholic who had found God and now spread the Word by writing 'Eternity' wherever he went), and was more than willing to take plenty of risks. Three decades before Britain's chat show hosts were hailed as 'bold' and 'innovative' for attempting much the same thing, Dave Allen improvised regularly on air in Australia, tearing up the running order whenever he felt like it, going walkabout in and outside the studio, holding impromptu conversations with members of the audience and launching into innumerable digressions about sex, death, politics and religion. He also seemed to relish the chance to try a wide range of dangerous stunts, such as the occasion when he attempted to tame twenty-five highly poisonous snakes, the night when he tried to execute a triple-somersault by means of a trampoline (he ended up being rushed to hospital after missing said trampoline on his way back down and then knocking himself out on the hard studio floor) and the time when he allowed himself to be strapped inside a car, then submerged inside a tank full of water and left to seek a safe way to escape. 'The only thing the audience couldn't see was the microphone – the only way that we could protect the microphone was to put a contraceptive on it, and as the water hit the bubble it was the last thing I could see before I went under.'[19] When he went back to Britain, he did so confident that he could cope with any challenge that television might throw at him. He was well and truly ready.

It showed. Bill Cotton saw him and signed him up to be the resident comic on *The Val Doonican Show*, a new peak-time Saturday night entertainment show that was set to be screened on BBC1. The first edition, broadcast at 9.00pm on 7 October 1965, confirmed Dave Allen's great potential: he was youthful, bright, assured and stylish, performing a mixture of material that managed to switch smoothly back and forth between the conventional and the controversial.

There was no one else quite like him on British television at that time; he had more in common with the current crop of American comedians, like the edgily contemporary Lenny Bruce and Mort Sahl (who found humour in religion, politics and big business), and slick observational humorists like Alan King, Bill Cosby and Bob Newhart. He was probably closest to George Carlin – another lapsed Catholic – in terms of his crafty blend of gritty themes and silky tones. Carlin's humour, like Allen's, could be refreshingly self-critical ('Have you ever noticed that anybody driving slower than you is an idiot, and anyone going faster is a maniac?'), smartly whimsical ('What if there were no hypothetical questions?'), artfully iconoclastic ('I have as much authority as the Pope. I just don't have as many people who believe it') and openly liberal and satirical ('There are 400,000 words in the English language,' one of Carlin's most controversial routines began. 'And there are seven of them that you can't say on television. What a ratio that is – 399,993 to seven! They must *really* be bad!') without alienating the majority of the mainstream audience.

Carlin, however, lacked Allen's elegance and subtlety, as well as his leading-man good looks. Whereas Carlin grew louder, angrier and much more antagonistic as he drifted off into a hippy-dippy hinterland, Allen bought an even better class of bespoke three-piece suit, as he charmed and challenged and entertained much of the nation.

The other fine quality that was evident in Dave Allen as a performer was his courage: he was not afraid of silence. Unlike the typical front cloth comic for whom the space between each line signified nothing more than a pointless waste of airtime, he refused to hurtle through all of his material at the same old breathless pace. Like the great Jack Benny, he was both able and willing to pause in the middle of a joke or a story, take a long look at the audience and share an unspoken thought. It was an intimate, urbane, sophisticated style that was ideal for a medium as inquisitive as television. John Ammonds, the show's producer/director and a shrewd judge of comedy performers (he would go on to direct

Morecambe and Wise through most of their glory years), was highly impressed:

> It was ironic, really, because when Bill Cotton had first mentioned Dave to me, and before I'd actually gone to see him perform in a club, I'd been a bit worried about whether he'd have enough material to fill each five-minute slot in a series that was going to run for eleven weeks. Of course, once I saw him do his act I realised that one story could take him five minutes to tell! So he was no trouble at all. I could bring the camera in, and he could draw the audience in, and then he'd hold your attention throughout what were sometimes quite long and elaborate jokes – and that was a real achievement. He was probably the one comic I'd known who could get, if anything, even bigger laughs at various points all the way through a joke than he got at the end on the tag line. He really did work extremely hard to get his material across, and yet he made it look effortless – which was the art, of course. So he was perfect for the show right from the start.[20]

Allen proved such a success, in fact, that he went on to be too much in demand to return for the whole of a second series. 'We tried to get him,' Ammonds recalled, 'but he was already quite worried about getting to be over-exposed.'[21]

The remainder of the decade saw him try out a number of promising broadcasting options. In 1967, for example, he revived the *Tonight with Dave Allen* format for ATV (winning himself a Variety Club award for being judged ITV's 'Personality of the Year'), and attempted another sequence of hazardous on-screen stunts: 'People used to watch the programme to see if I would kill myself.'[22] In 1969, he went to New York to film a fairly 'straight' documentary for ITV called *Dave Allen in the Melting Pot*, which looked at changing social and cultural trends in the US. It featured him interviewing alcoholics, drug pushers, panhandlers, police under-cover agents, psychiatrists and a range of social activists, as well as some 'Irish-Americans' who depressed him with their 'recollections' of the old country's 'thatched cottages, leprechauns and shamrock'.[23] He also ventured back to Australia, where he performed to packed houses, appeared on more shows, acted in a movie (called *Squeeze a Flower*[24]) and even released a spoken-word single – a somewhat whimsical but certainly sincere countercultural contribution timed to coincide with the moon landing – entitled 'The Good Earth':

> *When I was a child and the road was dark*
> *And the way was long and alone,*
> *My heart would lift as I turned the bend*
> *And saw the lights of home.*
> *Now high above in the silent sky*
> *In the still and starry space,*
> *A man looks down on the earth below*
> *And that blue and green shining glow*
> *To him is the lights of home.*

It's a good earth, yes, a good earth
A land of sun and rain and snow,
Of mulberry trees and mistletoe,
Of burning plains and raging seas,
Of Sunday morning taking your ease
And watching your children grow.

It's a good earth, yes, a good earth
Where we fought and loved
Where we killed and died
Where we ruined and ravished the countryside.
But now from a million miles away,
From another world that's cold and grey,
Someone is able to look and say, 'That's the good
    earth'.

So isn't it time that we stopped the tears?
We've lived together for thousands of years.
And whether I'm wrong or whether you're right,
And whether you're black or whether I'm white,
One day we will stand on the edge of the world
And someone will ask us the land of our birth
And we'll look in his eyes and quietly say:
'It's the good earth, yes, the good earth –
Why can't we be good on the good earth?' [25]

In 1971, however, he earned himself a lifetime ban (sub-
sequently – and quietly – rescinded) from live television
in that country as the result of a notorious TV special
featuring Peter Cook, Dudley Moore and himself:

It was a ninety-minute live show, and we had live adverts, and people would come on and talk about shirts or motor cars or saws or ladders or paint or whatever it might be, and they used to throw to these live. And I was there, as the host, and I had to explain that there was another advert coming up, and then they'd do them live. The show was going very well with Peter and Dud – it was really zooming along, it was really kind of clouting along – but we kept on getting these interruptions from the producer. So at one point I said, you know, to the viewers: 'I'm sorry. I'm very sorry. I know that you want to have a whole evening of commercials and we keep on interrupting you with this chat.' Which got a little giggle. And then, eventually, I got quite annoyed when he threw yet another ad at me and – John Collins was his name – I said to him: 'John, do me a favour, please: just down the back of the studio there's a curtain; just go there, masturbate quietly, and you'll be happy, and we'll be happy!'[26]

'I couldn't believe what happened [after the broadcast],' he would recall. 'It just *exploded*. The place exploded. I mean, the *audience* laughed, but from then on: the phone calls! I mean, there were old ladies fainting in Melbourne and throwing themselves off the bridge! And I left the next morning and flew back to London and found out I was banned from live television in Australia.'[27]

Back in Britain, however, he went from strength to strength, and the 1970s was the decade in which he arrived at his prime. His show on BBC1, *Dave Allen At*

Large, ran for five series and three specials over the course of eight memorable and successful years (from 1971 to 1979), winning a Silver Rose at the Montreux Golden Rose television festival and numerous other national and international awards as well as a large and loyal viewing audience. Written by Dave Allen with the assistance of his two regular collaborators, Peter Vincent and Austin Steele, the show featured its sit-down stand-up star telling jokes and stories about all of the classic comedy topics, as well as his troupe of tried-and-tested performers (headed by the diminutive Ronnie Brody, the large and moustachioed Michael Sharvell-Martin and the vivacious Jacqueline Clarke) in a wide range of deft and often refreshingly inventive light-hearted sketches.

The sketches really did matter to Dave Allen. There were plenty of comedians of the time who would don a different jacket and wander woodenly through a handful of weak routines, but Allen treated the format with far more care and respect. He shot about three hundred sketches for each six-week series, travelling to all kinds of strange and prosaic locations with the show's producer/director, Peter Whitmore, and a supporting cast that insiders described as 'a cross between a rep company and a commando outfit',[28] to film a sequence of routines that included a few quick-fire sight gags; some parodies of the likes of Robin Hood and his Merry Men, Sherlock Holmes and Dr Watson, several Shakespearean plays and one or two hoary Hollywood horrors; a recurring snapshot sitcom about a bunch of incompetent convicts; several extended sketches set in a post-apocalyptic future; and, inevitably, countless visual jokes about monks and nuns and a full quota of Catholic and C of E grandees. They were time-consuming and increasingly expensive to make (because Allen insisted on an approach that was 'fairly precise': 'I mean, if I'm doing a sketch about King John, I want it to be the real King John, not some cod, jokey version'[29]), but none of the team – and certainly not its star – ever wanted the action to end. Allen, in particular, not only relished the break from the conventional studio routine, but also enjoyed being part of a proper ensemble. 'He doesn't hog the funniest spots,' Ronnie Brody confirmed at the time. 'If it suits somebody else better, they get it.'[30]

Michael Sharvell-Martin, who shared so many scenes with Dave Allen, likened him to 'an older brother':

We became fairly close over those twelve years that we spent working together on the show, and we had a lot of fun. I remember, for example, when we were filming down in Bournemouth, doing a sketch about Irish pirates digging for treasure in the sea. It was February and really freezing cold, and we – me, Ronnie Brody and everyone – were up to our waists in the sea and absolutely frozen, but David appeared not to be affected by the cold at all. So we felt we'd better stop whingeing and just get on with it, and try to be as professional as David. Eventually, we all came out shivering, and he came out smiling and looking fine – but we then discovered that he'd had a wetsuit on the whole time![31]

Jacqui Clarke – his other key colleague on *Dave Allen At Large* – has similar memories:

They were my happiest times in television. Dave was so good and so kind, and he was always daring you, always challenging you in a positive way. For example, I'd learnt a really long script – pages and pages of the stuff – about the end of the world. And when we were driving in the coach on the way to the location, I saw Dave sitting there with his pen and paper – he was always like that, thinking about new ideas and sketches with his pen poised – and then, shortly prior to filming, he suddenly handed me these two pieces of paper and said, 'Look, I don't like what you've been given, just have a look at this and have a go at doing it instead.' So I did. Another time we were about to film a scene in this terrible old Morris Minor, and, after it had gone over a bump, he just said: 'I've just had an idea. I want you to be a nagging housewife – we'll stick the camera on the side of the car – and just keep nagging me about whatever comes into your head and we'll do something with it.' What he did with it was that the car was shown going over a bump and this nagging woman was thrown out of the sun roof! He often came up with that sort of thing at the last minute. That's what he was like. So bright, and so much fun, and very, very generous to his fellow actors.[32]

Probably the most popular routine of all was the one that featured two funeral parties caught up in an increasingly frantic Keystone Kops-style race to reach the last remaining plot in the same graveyard. It saw the two sets of coffin carriers walk briskly at first, and then run, side by side through a succession of narrow country lanes, then break off for a swift beverage at a local pub before resuming the contest with one of the coffins propped on a pram and the other one strapped on to the roof of a passing car. 'We were going through places where people couldn't believe what they were seeing – they didn't know that we were filming,' Dave Allen would recall. 'And we arrived in this little town where the graveyard was, and there were two women going: "Disgraceful! *Disgraceful!* Treating people's loved ones like that!" Then they watched while we humped this coffin over the wall!'[33] The darkly comic romp went on to be repeated on countless occasions, not only on British television but also on plenty of other networks around the world, and highlighted the fact that Dave Allen could still be exceptionally funny without uttering a single word.

The real heart of the show, however, was, of course, the sit-down comedy, when the cameras moved in close and Allen settled back, took a quick sip from his drink (champagne, in fact, not whisky) and proceeded to give a master-class in expert narrative technique and elegant comic timing. Even though he was by no means the only writer of his material, he was certainly the sole author of how it was performed (Dave Allen's God, in this sense, was always in the detail). Nothing ever reached the screen until it had been marked by all nine-and-a-half of his own distinctive fingerprints. Sometimes it was a sparkling new routine, sometimes it was a well-worn Irish gag, and sometimes it was something that was somewhere in between; but, whatever it was, Dave Allen always controlled the shape and sound and syntax, choreographing every last little stroke of the hair, sip of the drink, puff of the cigarette and brush of the clothes as he delivered the material so beautifully and believably 'as new'.

He was, by this stage in his career, as close to being creatively autonomous as any prime-time television performer could have hoped to be. 'I would never say that I "bossed" Dave,' Peter Whitmore later confirmed. 'I don't think anybody made Dave do anything that he did not want to do. He's a very strong personality. Quiet but strong. He knows what he wants, and he's always done what he wants.'[34] It was true: as far back as the early 1960s, when he had only just started appearing on Australian TV, he walked away from a hugely prestigious slot on *The Ed Sullivan Show* in the US after being asked to find material that the host deemed more suitable for a family audience. 'Most pros would have eaten humble pie and found another script,' recalled his agent Richard Stone. 'Not Dave. He walked out!'[35] The difference in the 1970s was that he was surrounded by the kind of people – such as the BBC's then Head of Light Entertainment, Bill Cotton – who were prepared to help ensure that his stubbornness would lead to something special on the screen. 'My job,' Cotton recalled, 'was to hold the ring, to allow talented comedians such as Dave the maximum freedom to explore their chosen themes.'[36] He and the BBC were repaid for their support with some of the most intelligent, mature and enduring comedy shows in the history of British television, featuring a performer at the peak of his powers.

Like all of the very best comedians, Dave Allen never stopped asking: 'Why?' He did not just tell jokes about alcohol, for example; he also asked why we choose an alcoholic drink, rather than a non-alcoholic drink, to toast someone's good health. He also asked why ostensibly grown-up and reasonably well-educated people need to be told to leave buildings by the doors marked 'exit'; why individuals with perfectly good eyesight will point to an empty chair and ask, 'Is anybody sitting there?'; why something is called a 'cargo' when it is sent by sea but is called a 'shipment' when it is sent by road; and why courts of law invite us to appeal to a book containing stories about dim-witted naturists, mind-altering fruit and loquacious snakes to vouch for our veracity.

It was not that Dave Allen looked down on the genre of jokes (he was, on the contrary, a great admirer, and exponent, of the unpretentious gag, and a few of his favourites have been included in this collection); it was rather that there was so much more to him and his humour than just a succession of semi-familiar cracks and quips. 'Thinking is my hobby,' he used to say, and it was certainly always evident that, whatever he did and wherever he went, he could not help but exercise his intellect.[37] An obsessive observer and note-taker, he would scour the media for issues that might serve as the basis of comic material, and was apt to wander around the towns in which he was performing, dressed anonymously in an old, well-worn mackintosh, to watch and listen to all of the people who passed around him. Jotting ideas down on old receipts, ticket stubs, theatre flyers, paper napkins, copies of *Scientific American* and little scraps of card – whatever happened to be closest at hand when the need to write arose – he planted the seeds of countless routines during the course of his casual travels. On a loose piece of notepaper that he had in his pocket, for example, he scribbled down some random thoughts and impressions ('Automatic doors . . . WALKMANS – NO CONVERSATION . . . Telephones – cars . . . Aeroplanes…Picking noses . . . necking in car . . . Lovemaking in car') that would end up prompting several observational monologues; while his memorable routine about the battle to give up smoking (which is reproduced here in full in Chapter 6) began life as the following hurried entry in the middle of an old brown memo book:

SMOKING

Good morning Darling
Breakfast

Drive us to school – Walk whining swine.

What time is it
Take your hands off my throat and I'll tell you.

HYPNOSIS – ASHTRAY – over smoke.
ACUPUNCTURE – STUDS IN EAR

Hands – life of own / Sex
RATIONING[38]

He loved it when such ideas leapt out at him from lived experience. Hugh Stuckey, one of the many writers attached to the BBC's Light Entertainment Script Unit who sometimes contributed bits and pieces of 'additional material' to the show, recalled how often a new routine was inspired by a chance sight, sound or encounter during the course of Allen's 'ordinary' life:

One day, Dave dropped into our office insisting that he take us to lunch at a special Chinese restaurant, the like of which he'd never seen before. He and the writers – Austin Steele, Peter Vincent and the others – often went out to lunch together, sometimes to Brussels where Dave knew a magnificent restaurant that had five Michelin stars. But back to the unusual Chinese restaurant. We got into his car, and along the way he built up our expectations for this restaurant. He'd never seen a Chinese one like it. He took us to Chiswick, pulled up outside, directed us to the door and proudly showed us the highly distinguishing feature about this establishment. There was a sign in the window reading, 'Closed for lunch'.[39]

His observations about the many oddities to be found among the minutiae of life had millions of people nodding their heads in eager agreement, but it was usually his treatment of the 'big' issues – such as sex and death and morality – that triggered the occasional tabloid-sponsored controversy. At a time when comedians were urged to err on the side of caution when it came to any topics that were considered potentially inflammatory, Dave Allen was a solitary but indomitable liberal voice, savaging the hypocrisy and cant of the media, the State and the Church and verbally cutting down to size anyone who regarded themselves as 'superior' to the common crowd. 'The hierarchy of everything in my life has always bothered me,' he said. 'I'm bothered by power. People, whoever they might be, whether it's the government, or the policeman in the uniform, or the man on the door – they still irk me a bit.'[40] He never let go: dogmatism and intolerance were mocked remorselessly in every show. 'Everything's guarded, everything's protected, and I fight against that,' he later explained. 'In societies, if people close you off and tie you down, there's nothing; you have nothing. You're locked; your brain is locked. And if they get that brain quickly enough and for long enough, then you're done.'[41]

Religion, in particular, provided the grit that created the comedy pearl. Roman Catholicism received the kind of shrewdly comical critique that came easily to someone who had grown up in the long and cold shadow cast by the Church in de Valera's Ireland, but the show's brand of anti-clericalism encompassed the full range of rival faiths. It was actually religious forms rather than sentiments, and organised religion's aristocracy rather than its rank and file, that were regarded as ripe for and worthy of ridicule, but the distinction did not always satisfy every worshipper who was watching.

In 1975, for example, Allen was reported to have annoyed a small minority of viewers with a brief sketch in which the Pope and six cardinals performed a strip-tease on the steps of St Peter's. The sight prompted Father John O'Sullivan – of St Wilfred's church in Northwich, Cheshire – to denounce Dave Allen during Mass and demand that he be removed forthwith from the BBC, although the Rt Revd Charles Henderson – the Auxiliary Bishop of Southwark – sounded a far more representative note when he stated: 'I do not object to jokes about the Church. If we can't laugh at ourselves – God help us.' Allen caused other self-righteous cheeks to stay unturned with routines that included coffins that moved like hovercraft, slyly flatulent bishops, priests who took bets, priests who beat up their parishioners, priests who beat up other priests, Dalek-like priests who conducted electronic confessionals and an extremely excitable Pope who spoke with a Chico Marx accent and ordered Allen to 'getta your bum outta Rome!' Sometimes, it seems, such irreverence led to threats of physical violence:

I did one religious sketch. The sketch basically was: a very old, decrepit priest – a bishop or a cardinal –

sitting on his throne and holding the crozier; and a nun came in and genuflected in front of him and kissed the ring; and then a second nun came in and kissed the ring; then a third nun – a very beautiful little nun – came in, genuflected and kissed the ring, and the crozier, just slowly, went into an erection. Which was a *nice* gag. And then I was in a restaurant two days later, and this Irishman came over and said: 'You take the piss out of the Pope again and I'll have you. Wherever you are. I'll have you!' And I said: 'What are you talking about?' He said: 'That thing with the crozier and the erection. Filthy. Disgusting.' And I said: 'Well, actually, if you knew the clothing, it was the Archbishop of Canterbury.' The man went: 'Oh . . . Ah . . . Ha-ha-ha – that's all right, then!'[42]

The complaints, however, were vastly outnumbered by the praise, and one admiring critic even went so far as to declare: 'What Lenny Bruce [. . .] did for sex and the four-letter word, Dave Allen has achieved for religion.'[43]

Dave Allen also did his bit, comedically speaking, for the cause of sex and the four-letter word. In 1984, for example, Mary Whitehouse, that doughty proponent of the doctrine of the divine right of self-appointed moral guardians named Mary Whitehouse, alerted the nation to the fact that she was most unhappy about a brief sketch that featured a post-coital conversation (and denounced Dave Allen as 'offensive, indecent and embarrassing'[44]). In 1990, however, he caused a far bigger and broader debate by using the 'F-word' on television at the conclusion of a comic monologue.

The monologue in question was actually a kind of 'repeat', in the sense that a much briefer and milder-worded version of the same routine had been performed five years before. In a show that was broadcast on the evening of 8 April 1985, Allen had made the following observation about clocks:

> I find it extraordinary, in this day and age, when you think of how a working man spends his life: he gets up every morning to the clock, he clocks-in to the clock, he leaves work to the clock, he comes home to the clock, he goes to bed to the clock, gets up to go back to work to the clock. He spends his whole working life doing that. And when he retires, what do they do? They give him a bloody retirement *clock*!

When, however, he decided to reprise the routine for a solo show to be screened on 6 January 1990, he resolved to give it a more elaborate and muscular structure, with a more powerful and passionate climax, and this necessitated, in his opinion, replacing the word 'bloody' with something rather stronger. 'The dreaded "F-word" was used [in the script],' recalled Peter Vincent. 'Dave stuck his heels in. And I looked at it and, in fact, there were *three* offending words, and we traded two-for-one. And then in the end, having traded two-for-one, it was transmitted in its original form!'[45] The routine (which is reproduced in full in Chapter 6) caused such a furore that a question relating to it was tabled in the House of Commons by a Tory MP who claimed – 'speaking as a regular rugby football referee' – that the language used by Allen had been 'worse than anything I have ever heard on the field of play' and was definitely not the sort of thing that any man should 'use in front of his wife', and the BBC was pressured into issuing a public apology.[46] Dave Allen, however, remained entirely unrepentant about the incident:

> I mean, 'blooming clock' wouldn't have worked, 'bloody clock' would have been only half as funny. We might as well invent a new word, glug, that you must not say. You send around an edict to publishers and broadcasters that the word glug is banned. And then I'd say, 'They give you a glugging clock,' and people would shriek, 'He said glug. How dare he say glug in front of the children who might be waiting up for the football?'[47]

He also vowed to keep all of his other expletives undeleted: 'I'm Irish and we use swearing as stress marks. Language is there to be used. If you sanitise it, you take everything out of it.'[48]

His audience remained loyal. They kept tuning in to watch him on television (there was another series, this time made by Carlton, in 1993), and flocked to see him in the flesh whenever he toured the theatres with his critically-acclaimed one-man show, *An Evening with Dave Allen* (which he never rehearsed but revised each night to ensure that it always remained fresh). His professional interests had always gone beyond the boundaries of the small screen – he had performed in a number of stage plays, including Edna O'Brien's *A Pagan Place* at the Royal Court back in 1972, and given a sneery performance of great guile as Captain Hook in the pantomime *Peter Pan* (with Maggie Smith) in 1973; in 1979, he played the central character – a lugubrious property man – in Alan Bennett's television play *One Fine Day*; and, in 1985, he toured Britain in another Edna O'Brien play, *Flesh and Blood* – so now, as the flat but snappy sound-bite replaced the well-told story in the forefront of cultural fashion, he was fairly happy to busy himself elsewhere. He consented to the odd interview in the broadsheets or on TV, but he remained as protective as ever of his privacy, and turned the talk into another seemingly effortless sequence of hugely amusing sit-down stand-up. Whenever the networks came knocking with requests to screen repeats of *Dave Allen At Large*, he thanked them for their interest but then advised them to devote the airtime instead to the promotion of new formats and talents. Although, in his own discreet way, he was rather proud of his past achievements, he preferred to stay focused on the here and now, and keep his comedy fully abreast of contemporary events. He never retired; he just slowed things down, spent more time indulging his deep and lasting love of painting (his first exhibition, *Private Views*, was held in Edinburgh in 2001), and enjoyed sharing more of the hours of each day with his family.

When he died on Thursday 10 March 2005, the immediate and profoundly heartfelt reaction of his colleagues and comedy peers, as well as the critics in the press and also the broader public in Britain, Ireland, Australia and various other parts of the globe, confirmed the sense that someone quite wonderful had just been lost: 'He was the uncle to end all uncles,' said his fellow Irish stand-up Dylan Moran, 'childlike yet oracular and possessed of a ravenous appetite for human folly. He could dismiss several schools of philosophy by shifting slightly in his chair or toting his whisky glass. When he adjusted his waistcoat or shot his cuffs, dragons of unreason gasped and died at his feet'; 'He was daring first and foremost,' observed another compatriot, Ardal O'Hanlon, 'and you felt daring watching him on TV when your parents were out'; 'He was an old friend but he was an idol of mine as well,' Barry Cryer recalled. 'He was so serious and committed, but he proved you could be serious and funny'; 'He influenced the world of comedy as a whole,' said Jack Dee. 'He was so sophisticated and cool and didn't need to act like a clown to be funny'; Eddie Izzard agreed: 'He was an original. He carved his own path. I think he was the first alternative stand-up to have his own show on TV, and he was a torch-bearer for all the excellent Irish comics who have followed in recent years'; 'He was just a lovely, lovely man,' added his agent Vivienne Clore. 'He was absolutely the same in real life as he was on the television. You always felt that he had made a special effort to know everything about you.'[49]

It surely goes without saying how greatly Dave Allen will now be missed, but it is good to know, none the less, how fondly he will go on being remembered. The recordings of his shows, thanks to the selections that are now being made available via video and DVD, will always be the first and best place to seek out and appreciate his particular genius, but there is also more than a trace of it to be savoured here. Clearly nothing can match the magic of seeing and hearing the man himself in action, but reading the ensuing lines and jokes and stories (transcribed from the proper final drafts – his actual performances – rather than just copied from the provisional scripts) can still evoke a precious echo of this great comedian's very special style and guile and grace.

What follows, therefore, is a reminder of what Dave Allen found funny: the ordinary things he and we did – on the way from cradle to grave – that underlined just how vulnerable, silly, trite, petty and wonderful the average human being can be. Smile at the stories, and smile at the memories: and may Dave Allen always stay with you.

G.M.

~

1

Childhood

*The world's a stage and most of us
are desperately unrehearsed.*

Sean O'Casey

~

'*I* have a reputation on television for being what we call a storyteller,' said Dave Allen during the very first edition of Dave Allen At Large. 'I've had this reputation since I was a child, in actual fact, because I used to tell stories about my brother and my mother and my father – I used to tell stories about everybody. I even used to tell the priest about the lot of them. He used to blackmail them – he was a rabbi.'

Childhood was one of those subjects to which he returned on a regular basis, celebrating its aura of innocence, wonder, enthusiasm and simplicity, as well as mocking its mismanagement by overly stern and illogical adults. The quick-fire sketches featured several instances of childish mischief (such as the one in which a kindly priest who, seeing a group of tiny children trying to reach up to knock a door knocker, knocks it on their behalf and then asks them: 'Anything else?' 'Yes,' shouts a little girl, 'run like hell!') and more than a few comical misunderstandings (such as the one in which a child sets off to dispose of her parents when told by the local priest that he is collecting for the orphanage), but it was the monologues that really mined most of the humour to be found in the memories of this early stage in life.

Some of the anecdotes and observations were drawn

straight from personal experience, such as his remarks about the myriad ways in which – right from the start – religion reached deep into the heart of the Tynan-O'Mahony family's life: 'I had an English mother, who was a Protestant, and an Irish father, who was a Catholic, and the priests used to tell me that my mother could never go to Heaven – because she was a Protestant and only Catholics could go to Heaven. And I used to worry about my mother, I used to say: "I love my Mummy, I don't want my Mummy to burn for ever!" And then she'd hit me for some reason or other and I'd think: "Oh, all right – burn then!"' *Then there were the tales about the excitement that was on offer each weekend at the local cinema:* 'It was on the Quays in Dublin and was actually called The Corinthian, but there were so many cowboy pictures on there that all the boys called it "The Ranch".' *He recalled how he and his school friends used to feed their early addiction to such escapism:* 'You'd pull dodges. There'd be eight or nine of you, and only one would have the money for a ticket, so that one would go in and then, as soon as the lights went down, he'd rush across to the exit door and fling it open – and hundreds of kids would flood in: "Scatter! Scatter!" The next thing to do was to pick up an old ticket: because, as you sat there, you'd chew it, and the usher would come up and point the torch at you and say: "Show me yer ticket!" So you'd offer them this chewed up bit of old ticket and they'd go: "Agh, filthy little boy!" Then we discovered that there was a method, if you were in the school lab, of getting a ha'penny and dipping it in silver nitrate, which made it look like a shilling. And this cashier at The Ranch was very short-sighted, so* *you'd give her this silver ha'penny and she'd give you eight pence change. They'd have a full house and they'd only taken about three quid!'*

There were also little anecdotes about his unconventional ways of keeping the youngsters busy during his days as a Butlin's Redcoat – 'I was a children's uncle for a while,' he recalled. 'Which gave me great power. Because you had these eight hundred or nine hundred kids to look after, and we used to have these hunts for things. Two of the things I used to ask them for were a penny – if they could find a penny dated between 1947 and 1949 or something like that – and a cigarette. So when you got eight hundred kids bringing back eight hundred pennies and eight hundred cigarettes I was set up for the week!' Countless routines would be inspired by observing the antics and habits of his own and other people's children.

He once drew a series of cartoons about a baby exploring his unfamiliar new environment. One cartoon showed the baby pulling the dog's tail; another one showed him looking for another building block to add to the ones that spelt out 'U-C-K'; one showed him poking an inquisitive finger up the dog's bottom; and another one showed him sticking his hand down into the bowl of the lavatory. All of these cartoons, however, were accompanied by a voice bubble containing the same adult admonition: 'No!' The sympathies of the artist were clearly with the baby, who was just as much in need of a 'Yes!' as he was a 'No!'

Dave Allen never lost the keen sense of fascination that came from reflecting on how odd the world could seem viewed through a fresh pair of eyes. The following selection, therefore, is a reminder of the kinds of moods and moments to which he often returned whenever he and we looked back.

G.M.

~

The Start of Stress

Have you ever watched a child in a pushchair? They're zonked – with stress! They're on the level of exhaust pipes, pumping lead and carbon monoxide at them. Have you ever watched a mother with a pushchair cross the road? What goes into the road *first?* Have you ever, at any time, seen a mother come to a crossing and *back* out into the road? They don't do that. The child is a test pilot for the safety of the road!

*

What about the mythology we teach to young children? The wicked witches? The Bogeyman? What about that for stress! Why do we inflict *that* on them? I mean, the Sand Man! We actually say to the young people we love: 'It's time to go to bed, because the Sand Man will come along at night and sprinkle sand in your eyes and you'll go to sleep'. Would *you* sleep after hearing that? Is there any adult in the *world* who would sleep in a house knowing that there's a bloody lunatic walking around with a bag of sand? He's going to let you have two handfuls in the eyes when he gets you! What about The Great Long-Red-Legged Scissor Man? Who cuts off your thumbs after you've sucked them and puts them in a bag! In Ireland, we had the Humpty-Backed Leprechaun, for Christ's sake, who'd put you in a sack and take you to live beneath the hawthorn tree! Jesus, I used to wet the bed! My mother would come in and say: 'Oh, look – you wet the bed! I'm going to tie a knot in *that!* Why did you wet the bed – why didn't you get up and go to the lavatory?' And I'd say: '*Ow-ow-er-aaaggh!* The Sand Man! *Aaaaaaagghhh!*' And she'd say: 'Oh! You are so *silly!* You're *so* silly. You are so *stupid!* There is no such thing as a Sand Man, or a Great Long-Red-Legged Scissor Man, or a Humpty-Backed Leprechaun!' '*Bu-Bu-But you said there were . . .*' 'I know I *said* there were, but I was only telling you these things so that you would have something to think about when you went to sleep! And even if they *did* exist, do you actually think that Mummy – *Mummy* – would allow any of these things to get any-where *near* her little boy? No. Now, I'm going to clean you up, I'm going to clean the bed up, put nice new pyja-mas on you, and then please go to sleep – otherwise I'm going to have to phone the police and they'll take you away and put you in a cell!'

*

When I was young, my mother used to discipline me through my absent father. I don't mean he was 'absent', I just mean he was at work. She would say: 'Don't do that. Do-o-on't do that. If Daddy saw you do that, Daddy would be very, very, very, very angry. Your Daddy does not like that'; 'Do not talk to Mummy like that. Daddy would not like it. It doesn't matter what way *Daddy* talks to Mummy. *You* don't talk to Mummy like that! Daddy will be very angry with you and he'll beat your bottom!'; 'No, you can't have another sweet. Daddy says too many sweets are bad for you. I personally would let you have another one, but Daddy says no. Daddy says they're bad for the teeth and worms will grow in your tummy and come out and eat the sweet shop!'; 'No, Daddy will not play piggybacks with you when he comes home. Daddy will be very tired – and you know what Daddy's like when he's tired: he gets *very* angry! And if he's very angry, he'll probably stop your pocket money and lock you in the cellar!' Now, my father, he knew nothing about this. He loved me. I *think* he loved me. But he'd come home and say: 'Hello, David! Give me a kiss!' *Aaaaggh!* I was gone! I was behind my mother, going: '*Waaaaagghh!*' My father would say: 'What's the matter with him?' My mother would say: 'No idea – he's obviously *frightened* of you.' He didn't know it, but he was a monster!

*

As a Catholic child, I was brought up believing that I had a guardian angel. This big spook with wings hovering around me all the time. And my mother would say to me: 'Did you do something naughty?' I'd say: 'No, I didn't.' She'd say: 'Liar!' I'd say: 'No, I didn't lie.' And she'd say: 'Oh, yes, you did – the curtains moved!' So I'd say: 'What have the *curtains* got to do with it?' And she'd say: 'That's your guardian angel going out the window. He's so disappointed with you for telling a lie he's pissed off!'

*

ALL YOU EVER HEAR IS ..

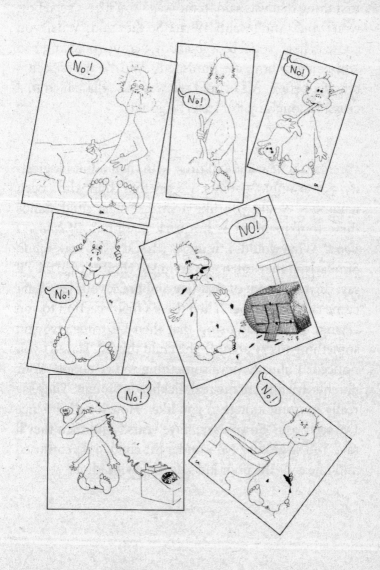

I arrived at this convent, with these Loreto nuns, and the first thing that was said to me was: 'You'll be a *good* boy, won't you?' And I went: 'What?' So they said: 'When you come in here, you'll be a *good* boy, because bold and bad and naughty boys are punished!' And I'd never seen a crucifix before. All I could see was this fella nailed to a cross! I thought: 'Shit! I *will* be good!'

*

Parents can bewilder children with their adult illogicality. For example, parents will say to a child who's been naughty: 'Would you like a smack?' The child stands there thinking: 'Eh? Is it a trick question? *Of course I don't!* Why would I want a smack? Are you *mad?*' Similarly, if they catch you trying to climb a tree, they'll say: 'If you fall out of that tree and break your leg, don't come running to me!' Then there's their reaction to you crying: 'If you don't stop that then I'll *really* give you something to cry about!' The child thinks: 'Haven't you noticed? I already *have* something to cry about!' Your parents' friends are the real dickheads though. They say really moronic things to you like: 'How long is it since I've seen you?' So you say: 'Five years.' And then they'll say: 'You've grown!' No wonder the child looks confused and uneasy – the poor kid's dealing with idiots!

First Confessions

If you're Catholic, you actually start off going to confessional when you're seven years of age. The first seven years of your life: it's when you've reached the age of reason, and you can tell right from wrong. The first time I went to confessional, I walked in and I didn't have anything to tell – I mean, I'm seven years of age, what have I done? Murdered anybody? Robbed anybody? Made obscene phone calls? – so I was making it up: 'I stole an apple . . . and-and I hate me brother . . . and-and I saw Mary Milligan's knickers!' And the priest said to me: 'Well, for your confessional, say two Hail Marys.' So I went out, and a couple of minutes later I came back and said: 'I'm sorry, Father – I only know one.'

~

First Confusions

My father did not like the word 'fart'. The first time I heard the word was when I was just a little kid. It was at a farm near us, and there was an old fella called Danny Dwyer who was a milkman there. I was watching him milking this cow with his hand, and the cow farted. I said, 'Danny, what was that?' and he said, 'That was a fart. The cow farted.' It was just a word; as if I'd said, 'What's that on the tree?' and he'd said 'bark'.

I had a dog called Tuppy, because I bought him for tuppence. One day, as I walked by him, I heard this same noise, and so I said, 'Tuppy farted!' My father said, 'Where did you hear that?' and I said, 'It came from his bottom.' He said, 'I do not want to hear that word used in this house!' Now, that's the surest way to get kids to say something – tell them not to. So I'd go out into the fields saying, 'Fart! Fart fart fart! *Fart Fart Fart!* My mummy farts! The dog farts! The priest farts! The Pope farts!!'

My mother never used to say the word 'fart'. She used to say, 'Whose bottom squeaked?' A grown-up woman talked about bottoms squeaking! My father also had a way of getting around the word. He would say, 'Who whispered?' And we totally accepted this euphemism in our house until, one day, my granny said, 'Come on, David, and whisper in granny's ear.'

*

I'm a godfather – which is a total contradiction in terms – of a child who recently went off to see a production of 'Allo 'Allo. And in 'Allo 'Allo he heard the word 'bugger'. He's seven years of age. So he went to his mother and asked: 'What does "bugger" mean?' She told him: 'Well, it's a funny word, but it's a rude word. And if you really want to know what it means, you should actually go to the dictionary and look it up. This is the way that we learn about words.' So he went off, he had a look in the dictionary and then he came back. And his mother said: 'Well, did you learn about the word? Do you know what it means?' He said : 'Yes: annual sex.'

*

I had an aunt in Ireland who was one of those fussy aunts. I used to go and sit with her every week and eat, and at the table she'd talk to me about digestion. 'You must eat properly,' she would say. 'It's very important that you digest your food. It's very important that you have good digestion. After every mouthful, you must masturbate thirty-two times.' I was just eating to keep up my strength!

*

My mother would say to me: 'Look at your face! It's filthy! You're a dirty little boy! I told you to wash your face!' I'd say: 'I did!' She'd say: 'No, you didn't! If you'd washed your face, it would have been clean. And it's not. It's dirty. You're just a dirty, filthy, little boy!' *[Thump!]* And then she'd go into her handbag, dig around and come out with an old handkerchief – a mucus-covered handkerchief that's been sitting in there for years – and she'd spit on this handkerchief and then proceed to wipe her spit all over my face. And she called *me* a dirty little bastard!

~

Early Disappointments

I'll tell you what I hate most: it's when a child specially asks Father Christmas for one specific toy, and you, the parent, go out and you buy it, and you bring it back and you watch him open it with great joy on his face, and there are no batteries in it. And you tear the box to pieces looking for batteries. And there, at the bottom of the box, written on a little piece of paper, it says: 'No batteries supplied'. And you try to get out of this by explaining to your child that Father Christmas has a tremendous amount to do: 'He's very busy – he's got all those homes to go to, and he's old, and sometimes he forgets . . .' And the little face [*Tears welling up*]. And you say: 'But, I mean, you do have *other* presents. Why don't you play with your nice big toy car that you got?' '*Eeyuwahh can't!*' So you say: 'But *why* can't you play with it?' And he goes: '*BECAUSE THAT DOESN'T HAVE ANY BLOODY BATTERIES EITHER!*'

~

Early Challenges

Have you come across something that says 'an unbreakable toy'? 'Unbreakable'. That is a direct challenge to any child! He's not going to play with it. He's going to try and smash it. He will spend hours endeavouring total destruction. And the toy at the end of the day is totally intact. The dog is dead. The mother-in-law is in hospital with major concussion. The house is in ruins. But the toy does not have a mark.

~

The Abuses of Enchantment

Have you thought of what we ask children to believe in at Christmas? I'm Irish, and I know that we Irish are superstitious – I mean, even our leprechauns are superstitious – but we actually ask our children to believe in an enormously fat, red-faced, sixteen-hundred-year-old man who – to make himself less conspicuous – dresses in a bright red suit with white fur edges, black shiny boots and a big hat with a bell. And for 364 days of the year he lives in the North Pole with lots of elves, gnomes and faeries. Whose total vocabulary seems to consist of: 'Ho-Ho-Ho! My name is Santa Claus! Would you like to sit on my knee?' And for the rest of the year we're telling them not to talk to strangers!

Not only that, but we also tell them that, when he leaves the North Pole on Christmas Eve to bring us our presents, his means of transport is a sleigh drawn by reindeer who fly! Guided by one whose nose is so bright that it equals the wattage of an anti-aircraft searchlight. And then when he gets here, he manages to break into seventeen million homes down the chimney. *The chimney!* Every house has doors and windows: surely that is the easiest way to get into a house? You open the door. Even a simpleton would know that. But not Father Christmas. This silly fat fart has to come down the chimney!

You look at the facts: In Europe alone there are nearly one hundred and fifty million homes, and he goes through the lot in eight hours. That means he lands on your roof, gets down your chimney, dumps the presents and is out in one-five-thousandth of a second! Are you surprised nobody sees him? 'What was that red blur? Ooh!' And in each house he has a mince pie and a glass of sherry! That means that he eats three *tonnes* of mince pies! And drinks nearly a million *gallons* of sherry! And then we don't see him for another year. Are you *surprised?*

~

Gender Stereotyping

If you think back to your childhood, we had very distinctive lines. Boys: you parted your hair to the right – if you parted it to the other side you were a poof! Girls: they parted to the left. We had our own buttons: boys buttoned from one side, girls to the other side. Our bikes were different. There were all sorts of immediate differences between the sexes. Little girls were soft and gentle; boys were hard and strong. Parents would say: 'Little girls are made out of sugar and spice and all things nice. Little boys are made out of slugs and snails and puppy dogs' tails.' And this used to lead to fights with your sister: your sister would walk up and go, 'I'm made out of sugar and spice and all things nice! *You're* made from slugs and snails and puppy dogs' tails!' So the boys would go: '*Grrrr!*' And she'd kick you in the groin! Then *she'd* start crying! And the father used to come in and he'd cuddle her because she was crying. She was *female* – it was all right. I'd want a cuddle: 'I want a cuddle!' So *I'd* start crying. *Smack!* 'What the bloody hell are *you* crying for?'

*

My mother was a great believer in what we would call sexual differences. I was four years of age, I would walk with my mother down the street and my mother would say things like: 'David, walk on the outside.' So I'd go: 'What do you mean?' She'd say: 'Walk on the outside of *me*'. I'd say: 'Wh-Why, Mummy?' And she'd say: 'It leaves your sword arm free.' I'd go: 'Er . . . What are you talking about? I don't have a sword.' So she'd say: 'No, but in the days years ago when men *did* have swords, some men might want to attack the female, so the *male* would walk on the outside of the female so that he could get at his sword and fight that person. You see? And that's why you walk on the outside.' I'd say: 'But-but I don't *have* a sword.' And she'd go: 'No! But you *protect* Mummy! You *protect*: you're a *male* – you are the *stronger* of the two. Males are the *hunters*, the *providers*; females stay in the *home* and make a home and a nest and keep it warm for the great [*Slap!*] *Stop crying! STOP IT!* Now, if a bus were to come up on the pavement, *you* would stop the bus from hitting Mummy!' [*Terrified reaction*] '*I* can't stop a bus!' 'No, but the bus would *hit* you and *stop* before it got to Mummy!' So I'd say: 'Up yours – I'm going on the inside!'

*

There's a child walking with his mother. He asks her: 'Mummy, what is that big house over there?' She answers: 'That is the house of God.' So he says: 'Does God live in that house?' She says: 'Yes.' He says: 'Can I go in and see God?' She says: 'Yes, if you want to.' So he goes in. He comes out again five minutes later. And his mother asks: 'Did you see God?' He says: 'No, God's away. But his mummy's scrubbing the floor.'

~

Zoon Politikon

Children are politically aware. For example, you'll get a child who goes to his mother and says, 'Mother, can I stay up and watch television?' And the mother will say, 'No.' So the child will go to his father and say, 'Mother says I can't stay up and watch television, and I'm asking you: can I watch television, Daddy?' And the father says, 'Yes.' So what the child has done by asking that question is to lobby successfully and cause a division against the opposition. He's also formed a coalition with his father – which is very good for the child, but the father is in trouble later on at night in bed when he is trying to form his own coalition with the mother.

~

A Swiftian Aside

Do you know one of the main causes of what we call the 'greenhouse effect' that we're all supposed to be going through? The loss of trees. And what causes the loss of trees? Babies. *Babies!* Bloody little crapping babies! Because babies use nappies, and nappies use up trees. Fifteen hundred nappies wipes out one tree. Over a period of two years, a baby, who uses six nappies a day, will kill three trees. Those little bastards should be got at! And who says we need all these babies? The Pope. It's his fault!

~

Prodigious Concision

There's a very good friend of mine who's a teacher, she teaches kindergarten children, and she sends me odd things about the kids. Recently, she explained to me that she was talking to these six- and seven-year-old children in her class about blood sports, and she put forward the argument that blood sports are very cruel. And then she put forward the argument that, maybe, they're not cruel – maybe they're necessary. She was trying to get these children to think. So she said to these children: 'What I want you to do now is to go back home and I want you to write an essay on blood sports being cruel, and I also want you to try to write an essay on blood sports not being cruel.' And she sent me this copybook that one of the little girls had filled in. On one page she'd written: 'BLOOD SPORTS ARE CRUEL!' And on the other page she'd written: 'OH NO THEY'RE NOT!'

~

<u>DA/103 (S)</u>

<u>THE PRINCESS WHO NEVER LAUGHED</u>

A STORY BOOK OPENS.

<u>NARRATION:</u>
Once upon a time in a land far
away there lived a Princess who
never laughed.

(THE THRONE ROOM OF THE PALACE.
(ALL DECOR IS STYLISED). THE
KING AND QUEEN SEEN TRYING TO
MAKE THEIR STONEY FACED
DAUGHTER LAUGH)

The King tried to make her
laugh. The Queen tried to make
her laugh. Even her little dog
tried to make her laugh.

(LITTLE DOG DOES HIS TRICKS.
NO CHANCE, HE GOES OFF WITH
TAIL DOWN)

The King sent for the court
jester, but even this funny man
could not make the Princess
laugh.

(COURT JESTER DOING HIS THING)

So the King, who loved his
daughter dearly sent messangers
to every land in all the world.

(MESSENGER ON HOBBY HORSE SEEN
ARRIVING AND UNROLLING A SCROLL)

And he made it known that he who
could make the Princess laugh

would have the hand of his daughter
in marriage!

(MESSENGER SEEN ANNOUNCING THIS.
SENSATION FROM HEARERS)

And in less time than it takes
to tell the funniest men in all
the world were arriving at the
Royal Palace.

(PEOPLE ARRIVING AT THE PALACE
GATES)

(THE THRONE ROOM. JUGGLERS,
CLOWNS, PANTO HORSES, COMICAL
ACTS OF EVERY KIND ARE ARRIVING
AND STARTING TO ACT)

But the Princess didn't even
smile.

(AMAZING ACTS HAPPENING WHICH LIKE
ALL THE OTHER COMICAL TURNS MAKE
THE COURT COLLAPSE WITH MIRTH.
THE PRINCESS SITS IMPASSIVE, EVEN
SLIGHTLY BORED)

The King became miserable. He
sat and brooded in the palace
and wouldn't speak to anyone.
(WE SEE THIS)

A FOREST GLADE

One day the Princess decided
to go for a walk in the forest.
She was sad. She didn't mean to
make her father unhappy. It was
just that she'd never seen anything
that made her feel like laughing.
Then suddenly, whilst walking,
she saw a man in the forest.

(GROTTY MAN IN RAINCOAT LEAPS
OUT AND FLASHES AT HER. SHE SMILES,
THEN GIGGLES, THEN ROARS WITH
LAUGHTER. WE SEE THE COURTIERS
WHISPERING TO OTHER COURTIERS AND
OTHER COURTIERS WHISPERING TO
PEOPLE WHO WOULD GO OUT LIKE
SOLDIERS OR COACHMEN ETC.)

The good news swept through all
the land! The Princess has
laughed!

(CUT TO JANGLING BELLS IN STEEPLE)

And in no time at all the Princess
and the man she met in the woods
were wed! The King was delighted!

(KING BEING DELIGHTED)

The Queen was delighted. And
the little dog was more than
delighted. And every morning the
very first thing they heard -

(KING AND QUEEN LOOKING UP
TOWARDS TURRET WINDOW)

- was the sound of their
daughter's laughter ......

(CUT TO PRINCESS IN BED. GROTTY
MAN IS FLASHING. SHE GIGGLES,
THEN LAUGHS AND ROLLS ABOUT IN
PAROXYSMS OF MIRTH. OUTSIDE
WE STILL HEAR THE LAUGHTER. THE
KING DANCES WITH JOY AND THE
QUEEN AND OF COURSE THE LITTLE
DOG.

- And the Princess and the flasher
lived happily ever after.

~

A Chip Off the Old Block

I was reading about babies the other day. Babies who get colic are given something called 'gripe water'. Gripe water is twenty-seven per cent alcohol. For babies. I was amazed, but then I thought to myself: 'Why should I be amazed – have you ever looked at babies? They're flat on their back, they can't speak and they shit themselves!'

~

Tempus Wotsit

We say to children that it's very important that they learn how to read the clock at a very early age:

'It's very important that you know how to read the clock.'
'*Why?*'
'Because it's important that you know how to tell the time.'
'*Why?*'
'Because how else would you know what time it was to get up and go to school?'
'*Mummy wakes me.*'
'Yes, but if Mummy wasn't there . . .'
'*I wouldn't go to school!*'
'How would you know when dinner time was?'
'*I'd be hungry.*'
'Shut up. You've got to learn because if somebody came up

to you and said, 'What time is it?' and you didn't know, you'd feel stupid, wouldn't you?'

'Well, why doesn't HE feel stupid? HE didn't know the time!'

'Shut up! You've got to learn how to read the clock, or the watch, or the timepiece – they're all the same, okay? Now, what we'll do is work off my wrist watch. This is a wrist watch. It's on my wrist. I suppose we call it a watch because we watch it. All right? Now: time is made up of . . . of . . . of periods. Different periods, different lengths, of time. Now, the main time periods we're concerned with are what we call "hours".'

'Ours?'

'No, not "ours". They don't belong to us. Not like our house, or our car or our Mummy. No: "hours". H-O-U-R. It has an "h" in it.'

'Where?'

'It's a silent "h".'

'Why?'

'I don't bloody know! All right: hours. Periods of time called hours, and minutes and seconds. They're all part and parcel of the time. Okay? Good. Now, in each day there are 24 hours, right? 12 in the day, 12 at night.'

'But—'

'I know I said there were 24 hours in every *day*, but a day is made up of a day *and* a night. When I say "Monday" I mean Monday and Monday night. Do you understand? I don't say "Monday night" because if say "Monday night" it means a totally different period of time.'

'But why—'

'Look, just *shut up!* Stop asking questions and you might

learn something, all right? Now, there are 24 hours in every day, and every one of these hours is represented on the face of the clock. Because we have on the face of the clock what we call "pointers" – hands that point towards the various hours. There are three hands: the first hand is the hour hand, the second hand is the minute hand and the third hand is the second hand. *SHUT UP! SHUT UP! SHUT UP!* Stop crying. Stop crying or I'll give you something to cry about! *Stop it* – this is all very interesting. Listen, we'll do away with the third hand, all right? We'll just deal with the fat hand and the thin hand, all right? Good! Now, as I said, there are 24 hours in every day and night. Okay. Now, every hour of these 24 is represented on the face of the clock. You see them? They're there. All the numbers are there, see: 1, 2, 3, 4, 5, 6, 7, 8, 9, 10, 11, 12. *12 because 24 would be too bloody big on your wrist!* Now, when the fat hand and the thin hand are pointing at the 1 and the 2 up at the top of the clock – you see the 1 and the 2? – 1 and 2 is 12. 12. Yes, it *would* be 3 if you joined them together. But when they're standing side by side they are 12. Look, there's a 3 there by itself – you don't need *two* bloody 3s on a clock! 12 o'clock, right? Okay. The fat hand and the thin hand are pointing at the 1 and the 2 – that means it's 12 o'clock in the daytime.

'W-*why*—'

'Look, you *must* learn about this, because if you do, and you show me that you do, I will buy you a digital watch!'

~

2
Growing Up

Oh, where are ye gone, little curly-heads,
That travelled across the say?
'Tis but yesterday, as it seems to me,
That I watched ye here at play.

Nora Tynan O'Mahony

~

*T*he thought of the shades of the prison-house beginning to close upon the growing boy, or girl, prompted some of Dave Allen's most passionate comedy routines. He was always quite open about his hatred of any attempt to make something straight from the crooked timber of humanity. He fully agreed with what his fellow Dubliner, Oscar Wilde, wrote about such hubris in De Profundis: 'Selfishness is not living as one wishes to live, it is asking others to live as one wishes them to live. And unselfishness is letting other people's lives alone, not interfering with them. Selfishness always aims at creating around it an absolute uniformity of type. Unselfishness recognises infinite variety of type as a delightful thing, accepts it, acquiesces in it, enjoys it. It is not selfish to think for oneself. A man who does not think for himself does not think at all. It is grossly selfish to require of one's neighbour that he should think in the same way, and hold the same opinions. Why should he?'

Why indeed: that was the kind of sentiment that earned Dave Allen more than a few nasty little slaps during his Catholic adolescence. 'I spent a lot of the time outside the classroom, because I would ask questions and get into trouble, and I was made to stand outside.' He recalled, for example, how, after the latest instance of his playfully *unorthodox behaviour, he was sent to receive punishment from a Mother Superior who was brandishing a thick wooden ruler: 'She'd say, "How do you want to be hit? On the open hand or on the knuckles?" You'd say, "The open hand," and she'd say, "You've chosen the easy option. You must never do that. As you've taken the easy way out, I'm going to hit you on the knuckles." But if you chose the knuckles, she'd hit you on the knuckles.' That was the kind of thing he tended to remember: being taught to fear the 'wrong' answer.*

What he remembered, and hated, most of all were the routine ways whereby fear was instilled in young people purely, it seemed, for fear's sake. He recalled, for example, the daily antics of the Dean of Discipline at his own school: 'The Dean of Discipline would patrol. That's all he did: he patrolled. All the [floors of the] corridors were linoleum, and we all wore sandals to protect the linoleum, and so when you walked on this you squeaked: squeak-squeak-squeak. *But when all of the classrooms were full there was no squeaking because there was nobody out there – except the Dean of Discipline. And you'd stand in this doorway, which was quite deep but not deep enough to stop your toes from going further out into the corridor, and you'd hear this:* squeak . . . squeak . . . squeak – *coming down the corridor. There was also the swish of the gown, so it would be:* swish-squeak . . . swish-squeak . . . swish-squeak. *So you'd be trying to lose yourself in the door, or push your feet back, or something. And where my classroom was there was a stairwell which led to the classrooms upstairs, and you'd hear this man come down the corridor –* swish-squeak . . .

swish-squeak . . . swish-squeak – *and he would stop, and you'd know he was thinking, 'Shall I go up the stairs, or shall I go straight down and then go up the stairs at the other end?' And he'd go up the stairs. Now, I'm in a state of petrification here, sweat pumping out of me, and then I'd hear him stop, and he'd start to come back down the stairs – because he would know that there were probably two or three boys down there – then he would stop, and I'd see the bottom of his gown and his feet, then he'd go back up again. And you wouldn't know where you were or what you were doing. You were wetting yourself with relief at one moment and wetting yourself with fear at the next! And these fellas knew exactly what they were doing. They were putting the fear of Christ into an awful lot of little boys.'*

Every grown-up bully, as a consequence, came in for the same treatment: withering sarcasm. People who told rather than taught; people who ruled through coercion instead of consent; and people who cared more about obedience than they did about trust and belief – these were his primary targets. Anyone who took young minds when they were still open and then slammed them shut was on the receiving end of Dave Allen's comedy routines. It was one of the main reasons why so much of his humour, for all of its general air of adult sophistication, struck such a chord with his youngest viewers: it always knew who the true brutes and bullies were.

He sometimes turned the tables, however, and spoke on behalf of all exasperated adults about the transient peculiarities of adolescents, such as the sudden transformation of perfectly fit, upright and articulate teenage boys into

stooping, shuffling, grunting, knuckle-dragging Neander-
thals, and the school boy and girl's habit of using a mobile
phone to ensure that no callow thought ever goes unspoken,
and the strange but widespread fashion for making every
single little statement of fact sound – thanks to an addic-
tion to the rising inflexion – like a pathetically plaintive
question ('My name's Lee? I'm from next-door?'). For all
of his own memories of individuals being practically erased
by religious dogma, he was also sharply aware of how easily
the contemporary image business, with its obsession with
form and indifference to content, was cultivating a fresh
congregation of conformists, and so he made fun of the
fashionistas as well. 'There're so many people trying to get
in your head when you're growing up,' he reflected, 'and
humour is one way of keeping them at bay.'

Freedom was as close as Dave Allen came to a faith.
Freedom to travel and explore; freedom to observe and
learn; and freedom to reason and reflect. He favoured the
full grand tour: 'I actually think we should have freedom of
movement. Why should we have to go to somebody else's
embassy and apply for a visa to visit "their" country? We
don't all want to undermine the State, destroy the economy
and kill off all the government leaders. There are people
who just want to wander around the world and see it with-
out a guide forcing them round a ball-bearing factory or a
kindergarten where they're teaching acupuncture.' He also
craved unrestricted sight of the big picture: 'Government
falls back on the old cliché that it's not safe for the public to
know these things. They use expressions like "in the
national interest" at the same time as slapping D notices

on all forms of media. Freedom of information simply doesn't exist here. That's not only undemocratic, it's unhealthy too.'

Although he was not usually one to offer unsolicited advice to the young, he did do so on one quite extraordinary occasion while working in Australia back in 1969. Backed by a decidedly woozy-sounding lounge band playing 'Greensleeves' as he intoned some lyrics credited to 'Martin and Kelsey' (but identical to the lines in Max Ehrmann's much earlier poem 'Desiderata'), he recorded a record (a kind of forerunner to Baz Luhrman's 1999 novelty spoken-word hit single, 'Everybody's Free [To Wear Sunscreen]') entitled 'A Way of Life':

Go placidly amid noise and haste, and remember what peace there may be in silence. As far as possible without surrender, be on good terms with all people. Speak your truth quietly and clearly, and listen to others – even the dull and the ignorant; they too have their story. Avoid loud and aggressive persons; they are vexations to the spirit. If you compare yourself with others you may become vain and bitter, for always there will be greater and lesser persons than yourself. Enjoy your achievements as well as your plans. Keep interested in your own career, however humble; it is a real possession in the changing fortunes of time. Exercise caution, for the world is full of trickery, but let this not blind you to what virtue there is. And many persons strive for high ideals and everywhere life is full of heroism. Be yourself. Especially, do not feign affection, and never, never be cynical about love, for in the face of all aridity and disenchantment love is as perennial as the grass. Take kindly the counsel of years, gracefully surrendering the things of youth. Nurture strength of spirit to shield you in sudden misfortune, for many fears are born of fatigue and loneliness. You are a child of the universe; no less than a tree and the stars, you have a right to be here. And whether or not it is clear to you, no doubt the universe is unfolding as it should. Therefore be at peace with God, whatever you conceive him to be, and whatever your labours and aspirations in the noisy confusion of life, keep peace with your soul. With all its sham, drudgery and broken dreams, it is still a very beautiful world. Be careful, and strive to be happy.

He meant the sentiments, but, on more ordinary and less mellow occasions, he preferred to convey them through comedy rather than homilies. One can see what he means in what follows.

G.M.

Education

Formal
School was quite terrifying. The first time you go to school. My father said to me: 'There'll be a boy at the school who'll want to hit you. The first day in school, somebody will want to hit you. Now, *that* is the school bully. All school bullies are cowards, and he'll only hit you if he thinks that you're frightened of him. So, if you hit him first, he will run away.' I was expelled in two weeks for being the school bully!

Informal
Sometimes parents can get the psychology exactly right. I was the youngest of three brothers. My father came back one day with a big bar of chocolate and he said to my eldest brother, Peter: 'Divide that between yourself and your two brothers'. Now, this was our big brother: he was going to take the major part. But as he was taking the wrapping paper off, my father added: 'By the way – the person who divides the chocolate is the last one to get to take a piece'. So now you've never seen a bar of chocolate measured out and divided up so carefully in your life! The bloody ruler came out, the scales – everything!

Religious
I don't know how people can be convinced to believe in an invisible God. I was educated by the Loreto nuns. I

73

went to the convent when I was three-and-a-half. I arrived at this convent, and there's a nun there, looking at me: 'Do you know what this place is?' I said: 'Yes, it's a school.' She said: 'Yes, what else is it?' I said: 'Um . . . a convent? A convent-school?' She said: 'Yes, yes – what else is it?' I went: 'Er . . .' She said: 'It is the House of God! God lives here!' So I said: 'Oh. Is he in the cupboard?' She said: 'No, no, He's not in the cupboard!' So I said: 'Is-Is he under the stairs?' She said: 'No, He's not under the stairs!' So I said: 'Where is he then?' She said: 'He is here! He's looking at you! He's downstairs, He's upstairs, He's in the playground, He's everywhere!' So I said: 'Well, he's a big bastard – why can't I see him?'

74

*

You're told that God is watching you all the time. He's everywhere. And not only is he there, all the time, by himself, but he's also 'three-in-one'! I remember, quite clearly, being told: 'He is Three in One. He is the Father, He is the Son, He is the Holy Ghost. Three In One. Do you understand that?' I'm *four* years of age! I mean, the greatest theologians don't understand that, but I'd go: 'Yeah, sure.'

*

I am what you might call a practising atheist. But I'm quite happy to be an atheist, because I think that, actually, God likes atheists better. We never ask him to *do* anything. We're not *bothering* him all the time, saying, 'Oh God, please help me . . .' And as a practising atheist there are certain things that, well . . . I travel around the world, and no matter where I go, somebody called Gideon leaves me this book to read. It's an Irish book because it says that it all began at the beginning. Now, there are certain things, when I read the Bible, and I *do* read the Bible, that I find difficult to understand.

I mean: if God has been there forever, what was he doing before He got to us? I mean, what was He out there *doing*? Was He sitting there going [*Rubs both lips up and down*]: '*Blubble-Blubble-Blubble*'? [*Yawns*] 'Hmm, bored today. What'll I do?' I mean, suddenly from nowhere He decides to create a world. 'I'll make a world! Yes, that's what I'll do! Rivers *[Pop!]*. Seas *[Bumph!]*. Mountains *[Ping! Ping! Ping! Ping!]* . . .' Whoosh! Everything's there.

'I want a garden. I'd like a nice garden *[Thwack!].*'
Garden of Eden. 'I hate gardening. I need a gardener. Spit
and dust *[Slap!].*' Adam. And he – Adam – never once
says: 'Where in the name of God did *I* come from?' I
mean, he's *forty* years of age! He has no childhood, he has
no recall, yet he doesn't say: 'How'd I get here?' But he's
quite happy. He just kind of trundles around the garden
working away. And God is looking at him, and he sees
that Adam is happy. 'I didn't put him there to be *happy* –
I'll put a stop to that!' And God, during the night, sneaks
down like a thief and steals – doesn't ask, doesn't request,
but *steals* – his rib. And from his rib, He makes Woman.

And Adam wakes up in the morning – he's a real
thickie – he's lying there, and there's somebody else! He
doesn't say: 'Where did *you* come from? How the hell did
you get here? Wh-Wh-Where did you get those *lumps?*'
He just goes out and goes gardening. And God comes
down and has a conversation with Eve. And He tells her
that she can eat of any fruit in the tree, in the whole
garden, with the exception of one fruit tree. He's talking
to a *woman!* He actually tells her not to eat of the fruit,
and then when she says, '*Which* tree can't I eat?' He says,
'That one over there.' He *points* it out to her! And then
He goes and hides, and she sneaks up into the tree, and
a snake comes down and has a conversation. A *snake!*
Now, if *I* see a snake I'll back off. If one starts talking I'll
crap myself! And the snake actually convinces her to eat
the apple. And she eats the apple. And when she eats the
apple she learns shame. That's what happens when you
eat apples.

Now, she's not ashamed that she's disobeyed God or that she's eaten the apple. She's ashamed *[points down]* of here – one part of her body. That's all. She just becomes ashamed of that area of the body. Now, why *that* area? Why not her elbow? Her nose? Do you actually realise that if Eve had been ashamed of her nose, every woman in the world now would be ashamed of their nose! You'd all be sitting here tonight with little nose knickers on! Men would be in nightclubs watching totally naked ladies with G-strings on their noses! 'Take 'em off – Oh! I saw a *nose!*' And *this* is the book that you'll go into court and place your hand upon and swear to tell the truth, the whole truth and nothing but the truth!

*

ROMAN CATHOLIC BOY: Our priest knows more than your rabbi does.

JEWISH BOY: I know he does – you tell him everything!

Romantic

A young man, looking rather nervous, steps into a confession box and asks the priest: 'Father, is it a sin, a mortal sin, to sleep with a woman?' The priest answers: 'No.' 'No?' says the young man excitedly. 'No,' says the priest, 'provided you just sleep.'

*

There's a tremendous amount of rubbish written about romance, especially in ladies' magazines. [Reads:] *'I looked into his steely grey eyes. They had that haunted, lost*

GOETHE
D⁺FAUST.

(P.M.) [Religion]

Jesus - Stable =

Miracles —

Angels Driven out - 1 33. 360 668) All male.
Angels   266 . 613 336)

Day of
LAST Judgement =

Oedipus = (Good to his) (Loved his Mother)

Limbo = Purgatory — Waiting room —

Remand *

Father God - Joseph - Jesus =

Three in One =   Limbo
                        Purgatory

[Various levels]   (Purgatory)

little boy look. I knew that he yearned for me with every fibre of his being. I closed my eyes. I knew that the moment had come. I felt his hot breath on my lips. His strong arms encircled me, and drew me close. I felt his heart close to mine.' [Looks up.] That's impossible. I mean, if you're standing in front of somebody the heart has got to be on the other side. This poof is standing behind her! Either that, or he's hanging upside down from the ceiling.

Sexual

I started going to Biology classes when I was about seven or eight. It was during the first lesson that the word 'penis' was brought up. The priest said: 'How many boys know what the word "penis" means?' And none of us knew. So the priest said: 'Well, I want you to go home today and talk to your father and find out what a penis is.' So I went home and I said to my mother: 'Mummy, what's a penis?' She said: 'Your Daddy's having a bath – go in and ask him.' So I went in, and he's having a bath, and I said: 'Daddy, what's a penis?' He pointed down and said: '*That's* a penis.' So I went back to school the next day and the priest said: 'Did anybody find out what a penis is?' And I said: 'Yes.' He said: 'What is it?' And I said: 'It's a dick, only smaller.'

*

It's extraordinary being brought up in a Catholic institution because they will never really say things to you. When I was about twelve to thirteen we began to have lectures on what was called 'self-abuse'. Priests would come in and they'd say: 'Now today boys we're going to talk about self-abuse'. We'd go: 'Wha . . . What's 'self-abuse, Father?' So he'd say: 'Er, self-abuse is when you have an urge to abuse yourself. Satan, er, Satan rears his ugly head and creates sin, and a desire to sin, and a desire to take pleasure in your body. And, therefore, you abuse yourself. You have this urge to do things to yourself.' And we're all going: *'Uh?'* We've got no idea what he's talking about. 'What's he talking about? He's . . . He's not talking about wanking is he?'

And then there was all the mythology that comes out about it: 'You do this, and you'll lose two pints of blood. Every time you do that to yourself you will lose two pints of blood. You're draining yourself of your life's blood. You'll grow weak, pale and anaemic – and unable to walk.' And I used to look at the old Pope, all in white, quite pale, being carried around and I thought: 'I know what *you've* been doing!'

*

YOUNG MAN: Forgive me, Father, for I have sinned. I can't stop thinking about sex. Every second of the day. Morning, noon and night. Just sex, sex, sex. But I'm frightened to do it, because someone told me that excessive indulgence in pleasures of the flesh makes you go deaf.

PRIEST: I wonder – could you speak up, please?

~

A portrait of the artist as a young man, circa 1957.

The Tynan-O'Mahony brothers – Peter, David and John – out with their dogs in County Dublin.

The career begins at Butlin's: 'At first, I hated going on stage, but after a time wild horses wouldn't drag me off. I was getting my first real taste of show-business, and I loved it'.

Peter Tynan-O'Mahony photographed his television
set as his brother, Dave, made his television debut
on the BBC show *New Faces*: 'The longest, most
terrifying three minutes of my life'.

Appearing as MC of television's *Sunday Night at the London
Palladium* in the mid-Sixties: 'Dave's doing a great job for us,'
said ATV boss Lew Grade. 'He's in the star bracket as a TV host.'

On *The Val Doonican Show* in 1965: 'He was really a lovely artist to watch,' Doonican recalled. 'I admired the way he told a story, his impeccable timing and the material was funny'.

Sketches from *Dave Allen At Large*: 'I hope that God
has a sense of humour . . .'

With three of his 'wonderful repertory company': Jacqueline Clarke,
Michael Sharvell-Martin and Ronnie Brody.

This handsome man: the sit-down stand-up in action on his own prime-time show.

Growing Up

Life Lessons

When I was a little boy, I used to what we'd call 'mitch' from school. Which means that I didn't go to school. I used to go to a station in the morning and carry bags and cases. And I used to get money for this, and then I used to go to the pictures in the afternoon. And I was in the station one morning and a fella who was a bit bigger than me came up and said: 'Anything that you get today, I get half of!' I'm a devout coward, so I agreed. And a priest came up to me and said: 'Take that case to the hotel.' Which I did. I took the case into the hotel, came back out, and there was the big fella: 'Give me half of what the priest gave you!' So I gestured half a blessing.

~

Phone Home

The telephone was our link with the outside world when I was growing up. When the phone rang in our house, we would all, as a family unit, gather around it, and then my father would pick it up. Some of the greatest events in the world I discovered via the telephone. I'm three years of age, and my father picks up the phone, we're all standing there, and he says: 'Oh, *dear!*' Then he puts the phone back down and turns to us all and says: 'Adolf Hitler has invaded Poland.' And everybody else went: 'Ohhhh!' And I went: 'Ohh?!' Another time: 'Aunt Alice is dead.' And everybody else went: 'Ohhhh!' And I went:

'Ohh!?' He said: 'The funeral's Tuesday so there'll be no school.' So I went: 'Hooray! Ha-Ha!'

It was a sneak as well, the telephone. It knew everything. It rang one day, everybody gathered around it and my father spoke into it, then put it back down, then looked at me and said: 'What were you doing in Delaney's orchard?' Bloody telephone sneaking on me!

And then, over the years as I was growing up, I began to deal with it in a better way. It wasn't such an extraordinary item any more. But I was still a little bit wary of it. I'd lift up the receiver occasionally and listen to the dialling tone! That's how far our daring went! We'd pick it up and it would go: *Brrrrrrrrr.* 'I can hear the dialling tone,' I'd whisper. We'd invite friends over to listen! You'd get asked the next day at school: 'What did you do yesterday?' You'd say: 'We listened to the dialling tone.' And the others would go: '*Really?* Wow!'

Then you'd get a little bit more daring. You actually make a phone call! You wouldn't speak – you'd just make a phone call. You ring up and someone says: 'Hello?' And you put the phone down and piss yourself with laughter! Then, like all children, you'd go through a 'rude' stage on the telephone. I'd just pick out a phone number, call it, someone would answer the phone and I'd just say: 'Willy!' They'd say: 'Willy who?' And I'd go: 'My willy! Ha-Ha!' So they'd say something like: 'I don't think that's very funny, young man.' I'd just go: 'Cow's bum!' They'd say: 'I think that you're being a very silly young boy!' I'd go: 'Donkey's dick!'

Then there was a point, when I was about twelve,

when we reached the final stage of grot. We'd all be round the phone, we'd have the receiver up off the hook, and one of us would say: 'Anyone got a fart building up?' 'Yeah, I got one coming!' So then we'd phone the priest or the police station. Let 'em have it: '*Buurrrruuumph!*'

It's at that stage when you think to pretend to be one of the engineers from the telephone company. You'd ring somebody up and say: 'Yes, hello, can I speak to Mr Wall?' And they'd say: '"Mr Wall"? Mr Wall doesn't live here.' So you'd say: 'Oh. What about Mrs Wall?' They'd say: 'No, she doesn't live here, either.' So we'd say: 'Oh. You have no Walls in the house?' They'd say: 'No.' So we'd say: 'How do you keep your ceiling up? *Ha-Ha-Ha-Ha!*'

It was amazing – the gullibility of people on the phone! I suppose the worst thing that we ever did was to call people up and convince them that *old* words from *used* conversations, past conversations, could – like air bubbles in a water pipe – clog up the lines. And we said that the only way that they could get rid of these words was to immerse their telephone in water. And these dickheads used to do it! We had one fella who said: 'Er, well, I don't have a bucket of water here. I've got a goldfish bowl – will that do?' Then we told them: 'When you've taken the phone back out of the water, will you talk back to us to see how the words are?' And we'd hear the phone going into the water – *whoosh-bub-bub-bub-bubble . . .* – and then about twenty seconds later we'd hear them trying to talk into it again – '*whishish-shany-shetter?*'

The Family Pets

My Uncle Barry, who was a barrister, died. And he had a dog, an Irish terrier, a wire-haired Irish terrier, called Paddy. And we didn't know it but Paddy used to go to the pub with Uncle Barry, when he finished in the Courts Sessions and stuff like that. And Barry was quite a well-known drinker and people used to put booze down for the dog, you know, a pint of Guinness, and he would kind of get his snout into it and then he'd lower himself gradually down and get drinking, so he was a kind of three- or four-pint-a-night dog. And somebody would throw in a couple of chasers as well. So when Uncle Barry died, my family inherited the dog and he was a real angry dog. I mean he was *angry*: you'd go 'hello' and he'd go *Grrrrrrrrr!* and you'd put food down in front and he'd go *Grrrrrrr-raaaagghhh!* and another dog'd go by and he'd go *GRRRRR-RA-RA-RA-RA-RAAAAGHH!* and a cat'd go by *GRRRR-RAH-RAH-RAH-RAH-RAAAAAH!* and he was grumpy all the time. And then one day we were, I think there was a kind of party at the house, and somebody put their Guinness down on the floor and he started to drink it. And then somebody else said: 'Oh, he likes Guinness!' So they were pouring out Guinness and suddenly he was the happiest dog. And what we didn't know was: he was having withdrawal symptoms!

*

My brother and I, we went across the river, there was a family across the river called the O'Tooles. They used to breed pigs. And the sow had had a huge litter of maybe eighteen pigs or something, and there's always a runt of a litter, there's always a small one, which is generally kind of gobbled up or destroyed by the others or whatever. So Mrs O'Toole said: 'Do you want the runt?' And it was lovely. I mean this baby pig, all little, pink with very bright pink eyes and everything – lovely. So we said yes and we took it home and we called it Paddy: Paddy the pig. Paddy the pig had never seen a pig. I mean he'd been removed from the other pigs very quickly and then he came straight to us where we had these five or six dogs. So he grew up with the dogs and he grew up believing *he* was a dog, because he'd never seen anything else. And they'd all run around and go *ruff-ruff-ruff!* and he'd go *ruff-ruff-ruff!* And he'd jump in the water and he'd race with them. He'd headbutt them. I mean, if they bit him he'd really bang them in the head and he was just a great character. And we also had Paddy the angry dog as well – so you'd call, 'Paddy, Paddy . . .' and suddenly you'd get this pig and angry dog coming at you. And sadly, in the evening, when all the other dogs were allowed into the house, we used to have to put Paddy the pig in the out-house and you'd hear *eek-eek-eek* – terrible kind of whining little noises from the pig. We used to try and sneak him into the house at night without my father knowing, you know, wrap him up and sneak him through, but he'd go rummaging around and he'd crash into things and they found out, but he was a great char-acter. And then one day he was too big, he was a twenty-eight pounder or something like that, crashing around, so we came back from Mass one morning and he was gone. So we never knew what became of Paddy the pig. I mean, I don't know if we had him for dinner three weeks later or somebody else did.

~

The Family Circle

I grew up surrounded by a series of Irish aunties. A collection of spinster ladies, all devoutly Catholic. There was Aunt Katharine. Aunt Katharine was enormous. Oh, Jesus! She had fat on her fat! Her breasts – I'm not joking – they looked like torpedoes! She sat down and these things used to rest on her knees and reach over the edge. *Extraordinary* things. I don't know if you've ever observed females as they walk: there's a motion, a movement, to the breasts. For example, when they put their left foot forward, the breasts sort of *swing*. It's a kind of displacement, a gravitational pull. They just go off. Watch a woman walk down the road – the breasts are actually going like that [*makes a sensuously undulating gesture*] – just very gently, very nice. Anyway, Aunt Katharine would walk down the road and with the first step she would start them off – her breasts would go into motion. She would go along and they'd be swaying, and they'd come back at an ever-increasing speed, and as she walked down the street, with these things going from side to side like that, you'd see other pedestrians being flung into the bloody road!

She was wonderful when she sat down, because she was so fat that she used to wear these dresses that rode up. Whenever she sat down her arse used to displace all the material. She'd spread out sideways and the skirt would rise up. She used to wear those very old knickers with the elastic that went right down there. In Ireland we used to call them 'wrist breakers'.

Aunt Alice was another one. Alice was locked up in her own mind. She was sort of trapped somewhere in the memory of her own past. I think she was about fifty-eight or fifty-nine at the time, but she always imagined herself to be about fifteen. There were times when she had to check that she was still looking like a fifteen-year-old: she'd take out this compact – she'd be sitting anywhere, maybe at the dinner table, at the time – and she'd open it up, look at herself, give a little cluck, and then she'd get the lipstick out and go round and round her mouth, then she'd get this loose powder, face powder, and she'd start going *pat-pat-pat* ... People would disappear for three or four minutes while she slapped her face a few times. She never smoothed it all down. You'd come back and there'd just be this lunatic sitting there with this huge half-moon of lipstick and layers of flaky powder.

Auntie Eileen was the nearest thing to an anorexic elbow you've ever seen. There was nothing of her. She was stick-thin and she had a moustache! Now, women will never acknowledge the fact that another woman has a moustache. I'd say, 'She's got a moustache!' and my mother would say, 'David, she does *not* have a moustache.' I'd say, 'She *does! She does!* She has a *moustache!*

Why doesn't she shave it like Daddy does?' My mother would be going: 'Shut up! Shut up! Shut up!'

Eileen had one big tooth. One big tooth, a moustache and myopic eyes – great big things – and she was half-pissed all the time. She went through about three bottles of sherry a day. I didn't know this at the time, I didn't witness it – she just always had this sweet smell. I'd arrive and she'd go, 'Oh, hello, Davey! Come over here and give yer Auntie a kiss!' And I'd get this great big sherry-smelling smacker all over me!

I also had an Aunt Cissie. Aunt Cissie had a nervous tic in her face. Two things set it off. One of them was our dog. We had a dog called Foxy, a little mongrel dog about sixteen years of age, and in all of his sixteen years he had never mated with a female dog. So by the time that he was sixteen he was totally frustrated, and had taken to screwing inanimate objects. He'd do it to trees, chairs, the back wheel of your bicycle when you were sitting on it – anything. I walked in one day and Foxy is humping one of the legs of the table. This was when my Mother showed me how smart she was, because I said to my Mother, 'Mummy, what is Foxy doing?' and she said, 'Oh, he's helping Mummy polish the furniture.' Anyway, the other leg that he really liked was Aunt Cissie's leg. She'd arrive, this lovely little Catholic lady, and Foxy would be on her leg, quick as a flash. She used to visit every Tuesday, and for about a day beforehand he'd be hiding behind the door, full of anticipation. She'd walk through the door and *whack!* I suppose, being a spinster and probably a virgin, she assumed that nothing was happening. She never said, '*Get off, yer dirty little bastard!*' You and I would. She didn't. She'd walk around the house with him on her. 'Oh, you've got new curtains there, I see' – and the dog's humping her leg like there's no tomorrow! This would set her tic off.

The other time the tic would go off was when they were all playing bridge. All of these aunts would come every Tuesday and they'd play bridge, and then they'd have tea at about four or five o'clock, and then at six o'clock the main reason for the visit would begin: poker. These five old biddies used to play poker every week. Now, if Cissie ever picked up a good hand, the tic would go off. She'd be sitting there, and this tic started going, and all of the other women used to sneak a look under the table to check that Foxy wasn't there screwing her leg, and then they'd throw the hand in. She never won a hand in all those years, the poor old lady!

*

I think that all of these aunties of mine had an agreement with the Irish Wool Marketing Board. Because any present they gave you was knitted. And they never knitted anything that fitted. They always knitted something you'd 'grow into'. Trouble was, by the time I'd grown into it I'd worn it out. They gave me all sorts – scarves, gloves, socks, mittens . . . The jumpers were the worst. You'd put your jumper on and these bloody arms would be down by your feet. My mother would walk around with a plate full of biscuits, it was like teatime at the elephant house! One aunt knitted me a pair of swimming trunks – which was fine until I went into the water. I came out of the water and looked like I'd got a great big lead weight hanging out of my trousers. I did hope I *would* grow into that!

~

Adolescence

Adolescents. They have this extraordinary ability to burn the candle at both ends. They have the capability of staying up all night. Not to mention the sexual prowess. Which is the same thing, I suppose. Their powers of recuperation are enormous! I mean, if I go out on the booze, it takes me three or four *days* to get over it now; I walk around with blinding headaches, amnesia, nausea, appetite's gone, bloody tadpoles running in front of my eyes! The young, they're totally different: they'll hammer fourteen pints into themselves – *whack!* – in one go, spend three hours in a disco jumping up and down, another hour trying to tell this female that the young man that's standing in front of her – this hulk with pimples, pissed out of his mind – is Adonis. They'll get home, they'll spend an hour, an hour-and-a-half, with their head in the bowl vomiting, *Bleuuugggggghhh!* Two hours' sleep. Then they're up again! Down into the kitchen: 'WHERE'S THE *FOOD?*' They'll sit there, and in half-an-hour they've gone through a box of *Rice Krispies*, a loaf of bread, a pint-and-a-half of milk, six eggs and a pound of bacon. Then they sit there finishing up, scratching themselves, belching, farting, saying: 'WHEN'S *LUNCH?*'

~

Curfews

Do you remember, when you were growing up, the curfew? You probably do it now as parents yourselves. You say to your own children:

'Be in by ten o'clock, all right?'
'Yes, Daddy.'
'What time did I say?'
'Ten o'clock, Daddy.'
'What time do I mean?'
'Ten o'clock.'
'Right. Ten o'clock it is. Ten o'clock. I don't mean five past ten, or ten past ten, or half-past ten, or eleven, or three o'clock in the morning. When I say ten o'clock I mean ten o'clock, and if you're one minute late you're in trouble. You'll be in exactly the same trouble at one minute past ten as you would be at three o'clock in the morning, all right?'
'Yes, Daddy.'

So you go out, and at a quarter to eleven somebody says: 'It's a quarter to eleven.' And you go: 'Oh, Jesus Christ!' Then you think: 'Shit. I may as well stay out until three o'clock . . .'

~

Young Men

What *is* it with young men? Up to eighteen years of age, they can speak perfect English: 'Hello.' 'How are you?' 'I had a very nice day today.' And then, when they get to be eighteen, their brains become haemorrhoids. All that ability to speak the language goes: 'Eeurrrrmmarurrrr.' They become Neanderthal men: 'Ugh-ah-muh-uh-muh-muh . . .' They even start walking like Neanderthal men. I watch them walk down the road *[staggers forward like a dazed and exhausted ape]*. I sit at home, Edward's friends are always ringing. I pick up the phone:

'Hello?'
'Hu-Ur!'
'Hello?'
'HU-A-UR-UH-HUR!'
'What is this – a yodelling competition? Apart from proving to me the ability you have to say, "Hu-Ur," what do you want?'
'Ur, UrsUhdUhn?'
'What?'
'Urs Uhd Uhn?'
'I'm sorry – what are you saying?'
'URS UHD UHN!'
'Are you saying, "Urs uhd uhn"?'
'Yuhs!'
'Fine. I know you're saying it, but what does "Urs uhd uhn" *mean?'*
'Uht Murns: "Urs Uhd Uhn".'

'Look, you know, I'm sorry about this – just bear with me,
     be patient – could you just do it a little more slowly, so
     that I can try to comprehend, all right?'
'URS. UHD. UHN.'

And I hear myself going: 'URS UHD UHN?' I think,
'What in the name of Christ is he talking about?' Then I
think, 'Wait a second: "Uhd" – "*Ed*"? Maybe! My son's
name is Edward. Maybe they call him "Ed". I don't
know. "Uhs Uhd Uhn?" – maybe he's saying, "Is Ed in?"
And I just try it:

'Did you say, "Is Ed in?"'
'Yuh! Uh Suhd: "Uhs Uhd Uhn?"'
'Well, you *didn't* say: "Is Ed in?" Dickhead. You said: "Uhs
     Uhd Uhn?" No, he's not!'

And the extraordinary thing is they have this need to
repeat everything you say:

'He's not in.'
'Huhs Nuh Uhn?'
'No. He's not in.'
'Nuh. Huhs Nuh Uhn?'
'He's out.'
'Huhs Uht?'
'Yes. He's out. If he's not in, he's out. I know it's very difficult
for you to understand that, but "He's out" means "He's not
in". He's not here!'
'Huhs Nuh Huh?'

'*NO! HE'S NOT HERE! HE'S GONE OUT!*'

'Uh, Whun Dud Huh Guh Uht?'

'*What?*'

'Whun Dud Huh Guh Uht?'

'I don't know when he went out.'

'Whunsurcumminbak?'

'I don't know when he's coming back.'

'Whur'd Huh Guh?'

'*I DON'T KNOW WHERE HE WENT! I DON'T KNOW WHERE HE WENT, WHEN HE WENT, WHEN HE'S COMING BACK – I'M HIS FATHER! I'M JUST A GERIAT-RIC OLD FART WHO KNOWS NOTHING!*'

And then he'll say to me:

'Ur, Whun Huh Curms Bak–'

'What?'

'Whun. Huh. Curms. Bak–'

'"When he comes back"?'

'Yuhr. Whun Huh Curms Bak, Wuh Yuh Suh Thu Nur Nur Rang?'

'*What?*'

'Nur Nur Rang.'

'"*Nyah Nyah*"?'

'Yuh! Uhm Nur Nur!'

'You want me to say to my son when he comes home: "Nyah Nyah rang"?'

'Yuhs Pluz.'

'All right, I'll do that.'

'Thangu. Uhs Bun Nurs Tukkin Tuh Yuh.'

94

And when I hear my son come in, I'll say to him: 'Hey, Edward: Nyah Nyah rang.' AND HE *KNOWS* WHO I'M TALKING ABOUT!

~

Young Women

There's a point at which your kids grow up. The girl will bring the boy home for you to meet. And because you've talked in kind of 'liberal' terms all your life, you have to follow this through:

'Daddy, I'd like you to meet Paul.'
[Grunt]
'Can I bring Paul in, Daddy?'
'Yes, of course you can.'
'Yes, but can he stay here?'
'Yes, of course he can. He can stay for dinner.'
'No, but I mean – do you mind if he *stays* here?'
'What do you mean: *"Stays here"*?'
'Stays in the house.'
'Doesn't he have a house of his own? Why does he have to stay here?'
'Because I'd like him to live here.'
'Well, where is he going to stay?'
'He'll stay with me.'
'What? In your *room*?'

And that's it! The bastard's in! And they take over. She loves Paul. Paul's an arsehole! I come down in the morning, he's drinking tea out of my cup. Reading my paper. Eating my food. And not only that, but he's humping my daughter! And I'm out in the garden, feeding her bloody rabbit!

~

3
Getting Started

*The most important things to do in the
world are to get something to eat, something
to drink and somebody to love you.*

Brendan Behan

~

*I*t can be hard work getting started. Take being a stand-up comic, for example. Probably every comedian currently in or out of work has heard the sobering tale of the prematurely cocky young performer at the Edinburgh Fringe who, after completing about twenty minutes or so of what he thought of as his strongest material, had still not managed to elicit a single laugh. As the saliva fled from his mouth, the cold sweat raced down his back, the cruel wind howled and the dusty tumbleweed rolled across the stage, the young comic played his final card. Spotting a mature-looking gentleman seated near the front of the small audience, the desperate comic called out and asked him for his name. The mature-looking gentleman gazed back at him and replied: 'Dave Allen'. The room fell silent as the rest of the audience sucked in and held its collective breath. The young comic, not recognising one of his profession's most enduring, successful and widely admired practitioners, pursued his line of inquiry. 'So, Dave,' he continued, 'what do you do?' Dave Allen looked back at the young man, paused for one, two, three beats, and then, very calmly and very softly, uttered the fatal words: 'I'm a comedian. What do you *do?*'

It really can be hard work getting started. Even Dave Allen himself took a while to settle into his own very *distinctive comedy style. He always told stories, but, during the early days when he was touring the unpredictable provincial clubs, he tended to rely on more impersonal and 'topical' humour to deliver the most desirable amount of laughter. A notebook from this time – preserved in the family archive – contains page after page of scribbled gags about girlfriends, wives and mothers-in-law, some longer routines about John F. Kennedy, Fidel Castro and Nikita Khrushchev, and some quips about James Bond, Bonanza, beatniks ('We had one of those people come to the door: "Aid to the Society of Beatniks". Dirty shoes, dirty slacks, dirty sweater, big dirty, bushy beard. She was a mess!') and dolly birds ('I tell you, those dresses are getting so short they'll soon have four cheeks to powder!').*

As he later explained, things began to change, and they did so very quickly, early on in the 1960s: 'I worked in Australia with a woman called Helen Traubel, who was a very famous Wagnerian soprano. We used to sit around, gag and talk and chat. She was one of the funniest women I've ever met. I'd be talking about Ireland, my childhood, my education, the schools, the priests, the nuns, climbing trees, all the kinds of things I did as a kid, and she said to me one night, "Why are you out there saying the sharp, spiky one-liners, attacking the world? Why don't you just go out there and reminisce?"' He took her advice on board, and drew more on his life to structure his act. Later on, when he had reached his peak, he would walk on to the stage with several possible shows shuffling away in his mind, and he proceeded to 'mix and match' in response to the mood of that particular night: 'I used to have a mental thing in my head. I had a structure of this skeleton, and I would say, "Right, tonight I'm going to start on the left hand, and I'm going to work up, and I'll go across the shoulder, and I can either go to the head or move over to the right shoulder and down to the right arm." I just had a kind of structure that I could wander around inside.'

He never forgot, however, how daunting it could be when one was just starting out, and, unless one was as spectacularly talentless – and precociously smug – as that hapless comic at Edinburgh, he always proved himself to be a good and responsive audience – and, if needed, a benign and compassionate patron – of up-and-coming writers and performers. No established comic performer was more delighted to see good new talent break through.

He also enjoyed reminding himself, and his audience, of just how vulnerable, confusing, exciting and frightening it felt back in the days before one could hide behind that carapace of experience, self-awareness and self-deception that we acquire once we reach that stage and age we like to think of and style as 'mature'. Dave Allen took us back in innumerable routines to that awkwardly intense moment when we first attempted to flirt, or anticipated our initial kiss, or tried to win the respect of our peers, or began a new job, or just drank our first wine, gin, whisky or beer – any thing or any event that reminded us of how it felt to be a fragile human being instead of a hardened adult. The beginner was rarely the real butt of a Dave Allen joke: even the young priest who is tripped up by his own halo when he sneaks a look at an attractive woman is treated with sympathy instead of a sneer; the audience is just left hoping that he *soon learns when to hop, skip or jump. Similarly, most of the routines included here invite a smile (or a shiver) of recognition rather than a sniggering sense of superiority. We have all been there; we all know how it feels not to know, or not know enough.*

Among the themes to be revisited is one's first experience of the kind of routine obscurantism that is passed off as transparency by religion, politics, bureaucracy, sociology and most members of England's upper-middle-class; the tentative negotiations that lead, or fail to lead, to intimacy; and the often ill-timed opening bid for attention. They will surely ring some bells.

There are also several jokes and stories here about getting to know the Irish, but they come with the affection of an insider, and the irony of one who knows how easily such affection can end up being abused by an outsider. 'You have to laugh at yourself, don't you?' he used to say to his English audience before launching into a classic Irish joke – then he would twist it around and use it to tease the English, whom he would then remind, 'You have to laugh at yourself, don't you?' He also understood how all of such jokes, at heart, are really not about other countries or classes or sexes: they are really about us, and our many imperfections, as glimpsed at and then hidden from in the mirror. The old saying, noted by Dave Allen, was this: the English may well tell jokes about the Irish, but if you go to Ireland you will find that they tell jokes about the Kerryman; and if you go to Kerry you will find that they tell jokes about the people who live in one particular road; and if you go to that particular road, you will find that they tell jokes about the people who live at number 46; and at number 46, you will find that they tell jokes about their father, or perhaps their mother, or their brother or sister – but, whichever one it is, you will find that the person reminds you, deep down, of yourself.

G.M.

~

Taking Things Slowly

A word like 'procrastination' takes on a sense of urgency in Ireland.

~

The Leap of Faith

The Pope is discussing the existence of God with an out-and-out atheist. The discussion starts off very correctly, but as the hours go by it gets more and more heated, and eventually the Pope turns to the man and he says: 'You are like a man who is totally blindfolded, in a dark-a room, looking for a black cat that is not-a there!' And the fella says: 'With all respect, Your Holiness, I think there's great similarity between us both.' The Pope says: 'Whaddya mean, "similarity"?' The fella says: 'Well, as far as I'm concerned, *you* are like a man who is blindfolded in a totally dark room looking for a black cat that isn't there. The only difference is that you've found it.'

~

Getting Your Bearings

Ireland
The Irish have always had a great desire to alter things. The first recorded Irishman altered the status quo of the

second recorded Irishman, who disagreed with him. He murdered the fella. The third recorded Irishman, bearing this in mind, decided to emigrate – setting a trend that has endured through to this day.

*

Ireland has one of the world's heaviest rainfalls. If ever you see an Irishman with a tan, it's rust. We have a very old saying in Ireland: 'When you can see the mountains, it's going to rain, and when you can't see the mountains, it's raining.'

*

The rain in Ireland actually saves many lives. It makes all the ammunition wet.

*

An important part of the Irish way of life is gambling, and you get these two fellas at the dogs, and one of them says: 'What do you fancy for this one here?' The other one says: 'I think . . . I think . . . I think . . . Trap Two. Yes, I think Trap Two for this race.' And there's another fella behind them, overhearing this, who says: 'I wouldn't bet on Trap Two if I were you. Trap Five is a winner. Trap Two is in there as a blind.' They say: 'D'yer think so?' He says: 'Oh, yes.' So they put their money on Trap Five – and it goes down and Two wins. So then one of them says: 'Now what about the second race?' The other one says: 'I think . . . I think . . . I think . . . Trap One, for this one.' So the other one says: 'Right, we'll put the money on One.' Your man's behind him again: 'Ah, no, One is a terrible lame duck. He's only there as a runner. I wouldn't touch him.' They say: 'You said that the last time!' He says: 'The last time I made a mistake. But *this* time: don't bet One – bet on Six!' So one of the fellas goes: 'What do you think?' The other one goes: 'Well . . . he seems to know an awful lot about it – we'd better put the money on Six.' So they put the money on Six, it goes down and One wins. They go right through the card like this – they lose everything. At the end of the racing, one of them asks: 'How much have you got?' The other one replies: 'I've got four bob.' He says: 'God, I'm starving – will you go and get two cheese sandwiches?' So the other one goes off, and comes back with two ham sandwiches. He says: 'I thought you were goin' to get cheese?' The other one says: 'I met that fella again.'

*

Which is the fastest game in the world? Well, it's played in Belfast pubs, and it's called pass the parcel.

*

Once upon a time in the south of Ireland, there was a man who made a lot of poteen. Do you know what poteen is? Illicit whiskey. And this man made the very best poteen in the world. Anyway, he had five very beautiful young daughters, and his last daughter brought her new husband home to him. What the man didn't know was that his new son-in-law was an amateur ventriloquist. And as the couple were riding back to the farm, the daughter said: 'Do a little of that ventriloquism for father when we get there. He's never seen anything like that before.' So when they reached the farm, it just so happened that there was a big pig leaning over the fence. The young man looks up, says, 'How you doing, pig?' and then throws his voice: 'Good morning to yerself, sir!' The father is there and he hears this. 'Did you see that?' he shouts. 'A dirty pig speaking English! What do you do for man, pig?' The son-in-law throws his voice again: 'I provide pork and ham, eat the rubbish and give birth to little pigs. I am a very handy pig!' The father is more than a little shaken by this: 'I-I see that. Goodbye, then, pig.' 'Goodbye, then, man!' A little further up, the daughter whispers to her husband: 'Do it again. Father's not quite convinced that the animals can talk!' And there's a big cow leaning over the fence – that's all the animals do in Ireland is lean over the fence – so the young man says: 'Hello, cow!' Then he throws his voice again: 'Well, good morning to yerself, there, sir!' 'Did you see *that?*' the father screams. 'The big *cow* talks! What do you do for man, cow?' The son-in-law throws his voice: 'Eat the grass, provide milk and butter and give birth to little cows. I'm a very handy cow!' The father is stunned: 'I-I see that. Well, er, goodbye, cow.' 'Goodbye, man!' A few minutes later, the three of them are at the farm, sitting at the table. The old man looks his daughter's husband over and asks: 'So: what do you do for a living?' The son-in-law replies: 'I'm in Customs and Excise.' The father tries hard not to show that he's worried: 'Customs and Excise, are you? A customs officer? Hmmm . . . if you'll excuse me, I have some things to do in the barn. . . .' So he runs out, digs a big hole in the floor of the barn, and starts burying the illicit whiskey. And, as he finishes, he sees a great big chicken staring at him. So he says to the chicken: 'You tell any man about this and I'll cut your throat!'

*

The Irish make perfect sense. It's just not always the sense that others are expecting. For example: you get two Irish fellas walking home one night, and one of them says, 'I tell you somethin' – it's a long avenue,' and the other one says, 'Yes, but if it were any shorter we wouldn't get to the house.' That makes sense, doesn't it? A couple more examples: A visitor to Ireland goes into a little country church and asks, 'Why is the bell ringing?' The man inside the church replies, 'Because I'm pulling the rope.' Another visitor to the church asks, 'Do you bury many people?' The Irish fella says, 'Only the dead ones.'

*

The Irish are often accused of being the most illogical nation in the world. Now, I don't actually think that we are illogical. I think that we are a nation of lateral thinkers. I don't mean we lie down and think about things, but we approach them from a different way. For example, I guarantee you that, if you go to Ireland and ask for directions, nine out of ten people will advise you not to start from where you are: 'I wouldn't start from here if I were you – go over there, it's nearer.' I'd been out of Ireland for a while and then I went back and I was in a restaurant, and on the menu it said: 'Goose'. Now, I hadn't seen goose on a menu in years, so I said to the waitress: 'How's the goose?' She said: 'I don't know, I didn't ask him.' I said: 'No, I mean what's it like?' She said: 'Oh, it's like a white duck only bigger.'

*

I watched a funeral go by once and asked who was dead. A local man said: 'It's the fella in the box.'

*

If you want to examine what some people term 'Irish illogicality', perhaps the best place in the world to go to is the courts. I watched a man in an Irish court – he was charged with some menial offence – and the judge said to him: 'How do you plead – "Guilty" or "Not Guilty"?' And the man said: 'Would you mind awfully if I listened to the evidence?' I saw a judge who said: 'I've reached a decision, and the verdict I pass upon you, the defendant, is: one year in prison and a £500 fine.' The counsel for the defence stood up and said: 'Your Honour, I'd like you to reverse that decision!' The judge said: 'All right: 500 years in jail, and a £1 fine.'

*

The English consider the Irish to be a very strange nation. For example, you get an Irishman who applies for a job at a building site. And the Englishman – a

Londoner – says: 'Well, we're goin' to 'ave to give you an intelligence test, aren't we?' (Extraordinary thing about Londoners – they're always asking questions: 'I went dahn the road, didn't I?' 'I 'ad a cuppa tea, didn't I?' *I* don't bloody know – why are they asking me?) So this Londoner goes: 'We're gonna give you an intelligence test, all right?' And the Irishman says: 'Yes, of course, all right.' So the Londoner asks: 'All right, darlin': what's the difference between a girder and a joist?' And the Irishman answers: 'Ah, now that's simple: Goethe wrote *Faust* and Joyce wrote *Ulysses*.'

*

A lot of people think that the Irish come over to England because of work, economics or even religious persecution. It's got nothing to do with that. The reason we come over to your country is that, over here, you are a permissive society – in Ireland we are not. Here, you have sex before marriage – in Ireland we do not. We come to get our share.

*

In Ireland, we have two types of Irish. We have 'Irish', and we have 'Anglo-Irish'. You can always tell the Anglo-Irish because they wear tweeds and carry shotguns. And they live in London.

*

If you can't laugh at yourself, what's the point? For example, here's a joke: Two Irish fellas leave Dublin to go to work in London. The collective IQ of Dublin halves overnight. (As I said, you've got to be able to laugh at yourself, haven't you?) When the two get to London, the collective IQ there doubles overnight. (I thought we agreed that you're supposed to be able to laugh at yourself?)

England
The English pride themselves on their logic. But I was reading recently where London transport have lost, in the last year, £40 million in unpaid fares. And I thought to myself: 'Well, if they applied Irish logic to that, they could save themselves a lot of money. All they have to do is to cut the fares in half and they'd save themselves £20 million.'

*

On the subject of the illogicality of England: if I decided – working on the assumption that some day we'll have a nice hot summer – to go into my garden and, because I like the sun, I decide to strip naked and lie in *my* garden, naked, and my next door neighbour – female – looks out of her window and sees my nakedness – actually sees my genitals, my 'privates' – she can phone the police and have me arrested for 'indecent exposure'! Can you imagine that happening to you? Your career is wiped out! People at the company that hired you would go: 'God, I didn't know that he was like *that!*' Your wife will wander around and the neighbours will say: 'Oh, poor darling! My God, imagine being married to a *beast* like that!' Your children will be harassed in school – all the kids will be going: 'Your dad's a flasher!' And yet if *she* goes into *her* garden and lies naked in the sun, and *I* look at *her* nakedness through *my* window, she can phone the police and have me arrested for being a peeping tom!

*

The English language is an astounding language. You think about it. You don't go for a drive in your car – you go for a *run* in your car. You go for a spin on your bike. And you go for a trip on a ship! We had a lot of trippers on our ship – they were falling over all the bloody time! You also go to football matches, where you don't stand in the stands. If you want to stand, you leave the sitting-down part of the stand and go to the standing part of the stand!

*

And the English are guided by the most illogical notices in the world. For example, in this theatre here tonight, the audience are informed by the management that 'when you leave here, you must leave by the exits only'. Now, I'm Irish – I don't have to be told that. There's solid wall and there's a gap. Go for the gap.

*

I see doors that have signs saying: 'THIS DOOR IS NOT AN EXIT'. In Manchester once, I was walking up this lane and on the outside of a door it actually said: 'THIS DOOR IS NEITHER AN EXIT NOR AN ENTRANCE –

AND MUST BE KEPT CLOSED AT ALL TIMES'! Why don't they just brick the bloody thing up and forget about it?

*

I went to a restaurant recently that had a sign on the front saying: 'CLOSED FOR LUNCH'. Schools now have 'green blackboards': I mean, why not just call it a greenboard? I saw a sign outside a school not long ago that said: 'SLOW CHILDREN CROSSING'. That's a great advert for the educational system, isn't it? I went by a driving instructor who had a sign in his window that said: 'Crash Courses in Driving'.

*

I saw a notice recently that said: 'Are you illiterate? Are you unable to read and write? If so, contact us at this address'! I go through Soho sometimes, and I see signs that say things like: 'LIVE GIRLS DANCING!' What do you expect – stiffs on a piece of elastic? I've actually seen by the River Thames a sign that says: 'This area is liable to flooding – if this notice is covered do not park your car here'. My favourite is actually the sign that says: 'HAVE YOUR EARS PIERCED WHILE YOU WAIT'. What else are you going to do – take them out and call back for them later?

*

And again on the illogicality of the English: the English for some reason or another seem to believe that they impart knowledge and information and understanding through proverbs. They speak in proverbial forms. Parents will say to children things like: 'Never cross the bridge until you've come to it.' And believe me: there is a proverb in the English language that actually states: 'Learn to cut your fingernails with your left hand, because one day you might lose your right arm.'

*

I mean, the English are really amazing with their language. I was looking for a house, I was trying to buy a house a few years ago, and every house I went into the people there would show me around and say the most obvious things. They'd say: 'This is the kitchen.' They'd show me, and there'd be a table and a stove and a sink and lots of plates and everything, and then they'd say: 'This is the kitchen.' Then they'd open the door to the lavatory, point at it and say: 'This is the lavatory.' The cellar: 'The cellar is downstairs.' Amazing!

*

Have you ever been sat in a bar, at a table with two or three empty chairs around it? Somebody's bound to come up and say: 'Are you sitting in that chair?' You'll say: 'Well, no, I'm sitting in this one!' And they say: 'No, no, what I meant was: is there *anybody* sitting in that chair?' So you say: 'Yes. There's eight people having a gang-bang – can't you see them?'

*

Have you ever sat on a bench in a park, and it's wet so you've put a newspaper down first to sit on? Somebody will come along and sit beside you, and I guarantee you that after about five minutes they'll glance down at the paper sticking out from under you and say: 'Um, are you reading that?' So you feel like replying: 'Yes – I have an eye up my anus. I always read it like that!'

*

When the English meet somebody who doesn't actually speak English so well, the only way they seem able to reason it out is to work on the premise that he's deaf! Say they meet a German: 'You want to go where? Well, you just go down the road. DOWN. You go *DOWN*. GO DOWN THE *ROAD!* Come on – *YOU FOUND BLOODY POLAND EASILY ENOUGH DIDN'T YOU?*'

*

I first realised that the English have a sense of humour about eleven months ago, when I was in Euston station. I was going home to Ireland by train – which is rather hard to do because there's a bit of water in the middle, but it was the Lourdes Express so we were all right – and when I got to the station I realised that I was short of my fare by three pence. So I said to this Englishman: 'I wonder, sir, would you be so kind as to give me three pence to get home to Ireland?' He said: 'Certainly, old chap. Here's a shilling – take three of your friends!'

*

"WE NEED A CLASSLESS SOCIETY" John Major 27 November 1990

Scotland

They say that if an Irishman is blessed with the ability to talk, he's kissed the Blarney. They say if an Englishman is blessed with the ability to talk, he's a politician. They say if a Scotsman is blessed with the ability to talk, he's sober.

*

You've got a Scotsman going to the match. A Rangers supporter. With the blue scarf, the blue hat, the blue rosette. And his wife goes: 'Ya look like a *clown! Ya look like a CLOWN!* Every day, every night, of each week of the year, ya think about *Rangers* – ya never think o'*me!* I think ya love Rangers better than ya love *me!*' He says: 'Darlin', I love *Celtic* better than I love you!'

Wales

You have two men talking in a pub. 'You know, I really don't trust the Welsh,' one of them says. 'As far as I'm concerned they are nothing but a country of streetwalkers and rugby players.' The other man takes offence: 'Oi – my *mother* is Welsh!' The first man smiles: 'Really? What position does she play?'

Australia

You know, I really love Australia, and I really love Australians. They are the friendliest, most hospitable people in the world. If you're thirsty, they'll give you a drink. If you're hungry, they'll let you eat at their own table. If you need shelter, they'll invite you into their own home. There you have it: beer, food and shelter – that's all you need. It's just those white Australians you can't trust!

New Zealand

On a flight to New Zealand, the pilot came through on the intercom: 'Ladies and gentlemen, we will be landing in Wellington in five minutes' time. The temperature is seventy-nine degrees. Please fasten your seatbelts and extinguish all cigarettes. Thank you for flying Air New Zealand.' Then he forgot to turn off the intercom. He turned to his co-pilot and said: 'You know the first thing I'm going to do when I get down? I'm going to have a large whisky, and I'm going to make love to a beautiful girl.' The air hostess is hearing all of this being transmitted on the intercom, so she runs up the gangway of the plane and an old lady looks up and says: 'There's no need to hurry – he's going to have a whisky first!'

Germany

English is supposed to be this 'universal' language, so why does it cause so much confusion when it's used outside of England? Take in Germany, for example. Saying 'Hello' to a German is like starting a quiz game:

ENGLISHMAN: Hello!
GERMAN: What is this?
ENGLISHMAN: 'How do you do?'
GERMAN: How do I do?

ENGLISHMAN: I, ah, mean, um, how do you *find* yourself?

GERMAN: I get out of bed effury morning and zair I am.

ENGLISHMAN: I mean, ah, how do you *feel*? How are you feeling, yourself?

GERMAN: Zat iss a very personal question vich I refuse to answer!

Divided by a Common Language

You should be aware of the fact that there are some peculiar contradictions in terms within the English language. If we are being aggressive or belligerent or threatening, we actually use words that imply friendship. 'Pal' is one of them: 'Listen to me, pal!' The Scots are always at it: 'You listen tae me, now, pal! You're askin' fer it, pal!' The Londoner uses 'chum': 'Awright, chum? Shaddup, chum! You wotchit, now, chum!' With the Mexicans it's always 'amigo': 'Hey, amigo! I cut your testicles off, amigo!' Americans are always: 'Hey, friend! Watch out, buddy boy!' Australians: 'Mate! All right, mate! You wannit, mate, you come out an' geddit, mate!'

And then, when we're actually being genuinely friendly towards people, we use the most insulting and derogatory terms: 'Hey! What're you doin', yer grey-haired old reprobate!' 'Allo, you old bastard!' 'Where 'ave ya been, you ol' pooftah?' 'You old bugger, you!' 'Ha ha, you're as pissed as a fart, you ol' bugger!' (What does a pissed fart look like, for Christ's sake? And how can a fart get pissed? What *is* a pissed fart? Does it wobble out of your bum and fall over?)

The Americans are never sure *what* they're saying:

they'll always use eight words where one will do. They'll get *lost* in words, and then they'll question you. Like they'll say: 'I had a cup of coffee. You know what I mean?' Eh? 'Yeah, I, er, had a cup of coffee, you know what I mean?' Well, shit, it's difficult, but I'm beginning to get there . . . You had a cup of coffee? 'Yeah!'

And the English always use expressions like: 'You don't say!' I drove the car from Glasgow to London. 'You don't say!' Eh? Well, who did?

~

Sending Out Signals

Have you noticed that nowadays, whatever you do, say or wear, somebody's trying to analyse psychologically what the whole hidden meaning or hidden message is behind it all? Scientists tell us that something like thirty-five per cent of all communication is made in words; the rest of it is made up in the way we dress, the sounds that we make, the hand gestures that we make and what we call 'body language'.

For example, we're told that we tell a great deal about ourselves and our inner selves by the colours that we wear. For example, people who wear yellow are 'basically depressed', and they're trying to 'brighten themselves up' by wearing yellow. Can you imagine that? 'Uhh . . .' *[Looks depressed]* 'Hmm, I'll wear yellow!' *[Forces a grin]* And they know, inwardly, that yellow doesn't suit them, so they become even *more* depressed than they were before they put the yellow on! I mean, if you wear *brown*, we are told, you're 'insecure', you're 'shy', you need lots of confidence-building. Grey: we're told if we wear grey we don't want people to know what we're really like; it's a kind of nondescript colour. *I'm* wearing grey. Blue: if you wear blue you're 'calm'. White: 'clean', 'pure', 'untouched', 'virginal'. (Why do nuns wear black?) Red: red, as far as women are concerned, is 'sexually aggressive'. That's what they're actually saying: they come into a room and they're actually saying: 'This is my *BODY!* It's *MINE* and I'm *PROUD* of it, and it does *WONDERFUL* things: *LOOK AT IT! LOOK AT IT!* It's going to take yours and *GOBBLE* it up in a moment!' And in a week she's wearing black, saying: 'He couldn't take it.' We're told that red, black and white are 'extremely aggressive'. Well, I'm wearing black, I'm wearing white, I'm wearing grey, I'm wearing blue: I'm calm, I'm virginal, I'm slightly aggressive and I'm not sure what I'm mourning but I *think* I know.

There's also, when we talk about communication, there's the body language. It's become now, in a sense, a 'science'. People actually believe in body language. There's all sorts of gestures, messages, that we send through our body. We'll be sitting very still, but our body is sending out all sorts of messages. For example, if I go like this *[Sits back with his hands behind his head]* it means I'm pleased with myself, I'm a smug little bastard. When it gets to folding the arms, folding the arms is, in a sense, telling you or other people to back off: 'I don't really want contact with you. This is *my* territory. Stay out – okay? I'm building a barrier – so push off!' This with the legs, when I do that *[Crosses his legs]*, I'm guarding the genitalia. That's what I'm doing: 'I-really-don't-want-anything-to-do-with-you-whatsoever-okay?' And if I do this *[Folds arms]* as well, I'm *really* telling you: '*Push OFF! You're NOT going to screw ME!*'

Open hands: 'Now listen to me. Please! Now *listen* to me! I'm being *totally* honest.' Open hands, open gestures. You sit with your legs open: it means that you're 'sexually available'. That's what it's saying: 'Honestly – I'm sexually available!' And when you do things like sitting in the chair, and you do things like *[stretches one leg out and idly wags the foot]* you're kind of pointing with your foot. You're inadvertently sending out messages to the other person that you'd like to have sex with: 'I'm sexually available!'

When you actually think of gestures – aggressive gestures – have you ever noticed that there're no aggressive gestures that are *down*? They're all *up*, aren't they? I mean, that: *[Thrusts two fingers up in the V sign]*. That's clearly aggressive. You never do that: *[Thrusts two fingers downwards]*. I mean, if you're in a car and somebody shouts at you, you wouldn't go: *[Thrusts two fingers down]*. It wouldn't mean anything. You've got to go: '*UP YOURS!!!*' All those signs, they're all *up*. Two fingers up. One finger up. Somebody behind you in a car blowing a horn: you look in the mirror and you go *[Shoves one finger up]*. You wouldn't put your hand out the window and go: *[Shoves one finger downwards]*.

Then there are things we're not supposed to do. When

the body behaves in a natural way. Yawning, for example. When you yawn, what actually happens is that your body is taking in more oxygen. But somebody somewhere along the line has applied what they would call 'rules': 'good manners' – 'you never yawn'. You go *[Leans back, stretches out both arms and opens his mouth as wide as it can go]*: '*AYYYYY-HUH-AY-HUH-HAH!*' Your parents go: 'Don't do that! *Stop* that – cover your mouth up!' So, when you have a yawn, you go *[Tries to keep mouth shut]*: '*Mm-mgh-mmm!*'. But at home, in the privacy of your own house, when you wake up in the morning, don't you yawn? It's beautiful. You don't sit up in bed in the morning, when the clock's gone *clang-clang-clang!*, and stifle your yawn. You go: '*Uh-huh-huyuhhhhhhhh!*' And your wife goes: '*Yeah-he-he-huyuhhhhhhhhhh!*' The whole house goes: '*Hu-yuhhhhhhhhhhhhhhhhhh!*'

It's the same with scratching: if you get itchy, you scratch, don't you? In your own household, you'll scratch. It's lovely: 'Ohhh, it's great! Mmm, a warm, marvellous thing!' It's body contact. It's marvellous. You'll actually get other members of your family to scratch you: 'Scratch, scratch, scratch – there! – down, down, down – oh! – up! – oh! – over, over, over!' And yet in public we're not *allowed* to scratch. We're not allowed to make contact with our bodies. You find yourself going to talk to your bank manager about borrowing money, and, in the middle of a discussion about rates and interest, you get a little itch half-way up your leg. You won't go: 'Excuse me, I have an itch: I am about to scratch it, all right? There's nothing filthy or dirty or unkempt. I happen to have an itch *there*.' You don't do that. You sit there, and the itch begins to spread, you get your hand in your pocket, and if you have to stifle a yawn at the same time it looks as if you're having a fit!

~

Getting Intimate

There's a point in every man's life when you buy your first contraceptive. Well, maybe not so much in the lives of *Irish* men, but there's a point in *most* men's lives when you buy your first contraceptive. And the most amazing thing about the first contraceptive that we buy is that we don't use it. I mean, we open it up and we blow it up and it goes *whooooosh* and you think, 'Christ – what does *that* fit?' But then you put it back and keep it in your wallet. And then over the years, that little circle makes a kind of imprint in the leather. You might eventually throw the actual contraceptive away but the imprint is always there. Nice memories.

*

Movies aren't realistic about sex. Watch a movie and you'll end up with a wildly inaccurate idea as to how sex works. Take that Michael Douglas movie, *Fatal Attraction*. I just don't believe the sex scenes in that. Remember when they go up in the lift together? They can't get off each other. They suddenly go: *Huuh-Uhh-*

Hu-Hurrr! They're at each other. And the lift arrives, the doors open, they get in, he picks her up and he drops her on his dick! *DONK!* Like it's a maypole or something! They didn't even have to search around – it was just up and in! *DONK!* And then he walks around the apartment with her stuck on his dick like that! I probably couldn't even lift a woman up! And if I dropped her on my dick it'd never work again!

*

You get the young man who meets the young lady at the debutantes' ball. He says: 'You don't know me, but my name is Fortescue Robinson-Smythe, and I have a reputation for being one of the fastest lovers in the whole of England. I'm *terribly* fast. And I've taken a fancy to you, little dolly girl, and I'm going to seduce you.' She says: 'Will I enjoy it?' He says: 'Didn't you?'

*

I had a friend of mine who was a very nice fella but terribly shy of girls. He could never talk to girls. And he said to me one night: 'I'm going to a party.' And I said: 'Well, good.' He said: 'But how am I going to talk to the girls? I-I can't *talk* to them.' So I said: 'Well, get a few belts into you. Get a couple of large Scotches in.' He said: 'But I don't drink.' I said: 'Try it – just try it.' So he tried it: *glug-glug-glug!* A different man! He walked into the party. The arrogance! The confidence! He walked up to the most beautiful girl there *[Clicks fingers]* and said: 'You and I are going to make love tonight!' And she said: 'Your place or mine?' He said: 'Well, if you're going to make a thing about it, forget it!'

*

A farmer has three daughters – the youngest one beautiful, the middle one pretty and the oldest one ugly. One day, when the farmer is away, a travelling salesman – a very good-looking young man – stops by and asks if he can spend the night. 'Do you think we should?' asks the oldest. 'Father isn't at home.' The middle daughter says: 'Who cares? Nothing is going to happen.' The youngest daughter just smiles. So the sisters decide to let this very handsome young man stay the night. After they've showed him to his room, the oldest one asks: 'What if he *does* try something? Shouldn't we have a code or something?' 'Oh, you mean like a secret word?' says the youngest sister. The oldest one replies: 'Yes, but what should it be?' The middle sister says: 'I know: for every kiss he gives us we'll say "Morning" to each other at breakfast.' So they all agree to do that. The next morning, the youngest sister is first in the kitchen. When the middle sister enters, she says: 'Good morning, this morning! A fine morning!' The youngest replies: 'What a wonderful morning this morning is! I have never seen such a beautiful morning as this morning! It truly is a morning of all the mornings I have had in many a morning!' Then the oldest sister walks in and says: 'Lousy day.'

*

You get a fella who arrives on the golf course, goes to the steward and says: 'Do you have anybody here I can play with?' The steward says: 'There's nobody here today except that young lady down there on the putting green. Go and ask her if you like.' So the fella goes down and he says: 'Excuse me, Miss, I'm on my own, would you like to play a game of golf with me?' She says: 'I'd love to.' So they proceed to play. It's a beautiful day, the sun is shining, the birds are twittering and they're playing marvellous golf. And they get to the last hole, which is a short hole, and he says to her: 'This is the best day I've had in years! Super day! You've been super company, and we've both played great golf. I'll tell you what: if I play this last hole to par, I will take you out tonight to any theatre you wish to go to, any restaurant, disco – the whole evening on me, because I've enjoyed your company so much.' And she says: 'I'll tell you what: because I've enjoyed *your* company so much, if *I* play this last hole to par, not only will I go out to the theatre with you, restaurant with you, disco with you, but when we're finished we will come back to my apartment – soft lights, sweet music – and we will allow the mood of the evening to carry us on.' So he says: 'Fine!' He puts the ball down: *voom!* She puts the ball down: *voom!* They get to the green: he's down in one, she is in the bunker. He says: 'I'll give you that.'

*

A Mother Superior is sitting alone in the convent when she hears a knock at the door. Opening it, she is stunned to see two leprechauns standing there. 'Excuse me, Mother,' one of the little fellas says, 'but would you happen to have a nun here that's about three feet tall?'

'No,' replies the Mother Superior. 'No, we don't.' The same leprechaun asks: 'Then, er, would you happen to have a nun here that's *four* feet tall?' The Mother Superior shakes her head: 'No. All of our nuns are five feet or taller.' So the other leprechaun nudges the first one and says: 'You see, there, O'Malley? You've been doin' it with penguins again, haven't you?'

*

You get the two women talking to one another and one of them says, 'I say – isn't that Mr Carruthers across the road?' 'Yes.' She says, 'Doesn't he dress nicely?' The other says, 'Yes. And very quickly, too.'

*

Then you get the young lady who has been seduced for the very first time – ever – in the back of a motor car, or anywhere else for that matter, and she begins to weep for things lost. The man says, 'Darling, don't cry!' She says, 'What do you mean, "Don't cry," you *beast*, you-you *man-beast*, you! It's all very well for *you* to say "Don't cry". *I've* got to go home and tell my mummy and my daddy that I have been seduced – twice!' He said, 'I've only done it once!' She said, 'You're going to do it again, aren't you?'

*

The Catholic Church offers to Catholic women the choice of two things only: perpetual virginity or perpetual pregnancy.

*

You get the two English gentlemen talking to one another, and one turns to the other and says: 'I don't really understand it. You see, I'm Church of England and you are Roman Catholic; I, as C of E, am allowed to practise birth control, you, as RC, are not; I have nine children, you have none. Why do you think this is?' The other man says: 'Well, you see, I only do it during the safe period.' 'Really? When's that?' The other man says: 'When you're at work.'

*

There's a nun. She gets up in the morning, and leaves and walks down the corridor. And another nun looks at her and says: 'You got out of the wrong side of the bed this morning.' She goes on down the corridor, and another nun says: 'You got out of the wrong side of the bed this morning.' And this happens fifteen times, and by then she's livid. And she meets the Mother Superior, and the Mother Superior is just about to open her mouth and the sister says: '*DON'T TELL ME THAT I GOT OUT OF THE WRONG SIDE OF THE BED THIS MORNING!*' And the Mother Superior says: 'I wasn't going to say that. I was just going to say, "What are you doing with the Bishop's shoes on?"'

*

There's the story of a young Church of Ireland vicar who gets sent to a new parish in the west coast of Ireland. It's a very large parish, and the roads are very craggy, so he has to cycle around. And occasionally, when he's cycling around this parish, he meets the old Catholic priest. And they're on nodding terms – they say things like, 'How are you?'; 'It's a lovely day, have you been fishing?'; 'How's the parish?'; 'Do you enjoy the Church?'; and so on. This goes on for months. But one day, the Catholic priest is cycling along and he comes across the Church of Ireland vicar walking, so he asks him, 'What happened to your bike?' The vicar says, 'It got stolen.' The priest says, 'Did it? Well, the same thing happened to me a number of years ago, and what I did, on the following Sunday, I prepared my sermon around the Ten Commandments, making special emphasis on "THOU SHALT NOT STEAL". And about a day later, when I came out of the vestry, there's my bike. So what I would advise you to do is: on Sunday, address your sermon around the Ten Commandments. Remember: place special emphasis on "THOU SHALT NOT STEAL".' And a week later, the old priest is cycling along and, coming up the road, on his bike, is the young Church of Ireland vicar. The priest says: 'It worked! The Ten Commandments! "Thou Shalt Not Steal"!' The vicar replies: 'Well, not exactly. It was when I got to "Thou Shalt Not Commit Adultery" that I remembered where I'd left it!'

*

There were two Irish fellas talking about sex before marriage and one of them turns to the other and says, 'What do you think about sex before marriage?' He said, 'I don't think about it.' 'Well, I know I never had sex with my wife before we were married. Did you?' He says, 'I've no idea – what's her name?'

*

WOMAN: Timothy . . .
MAN: Yes?
WOMAN: Why do you find me so attractive, Timothy? Is it my figure?
MAN: No.
WOMAN: Is it my complexion?
MAN: No.
WOMAN: My conversation?
MAN: No.
WOMAN: I give in.
MAN: That's it.

*

I overheard this young woman saying that her partner suffered from 'premature matriculation'. I was trying to figure out what she meant. Did he pass out quickly?

~

Getting Sexist

Have you ever noticed, if you compare animals to humans, sex rears its ugly head? What is normally complimentary to a male becomes a total insult to a female. For example, if you say of a male, 'He's a ram,' you think of great sexual prowess: 'He's a *ram!*' '*Bull!*' 'He's a real *stag!*' 'He's a *stallion!*' All highly complimentary. But when you get the female of the species and apply it to a woman: 'Cow!' There's nothing nice about being called a cow: 'Fat cow!' 'You stupid old cow!' If you say of somebody, 'He's a gay dog,' you're thinking of somebody who's *[Affects a mischievous Terry-Thomas look]*. But then they say: 'She's a bitch!' – she's sly, she's sneaky. 'Fox': you think of a fox as clever, sharp, intelligent. 'Vixen': mean, crafty. It isn't fair!

~

Making Your Name

There was this young priest who was fast acquiring a reputation for being a great inspirational speaker. And the Bishop hears of him and says: 'I want you to speak to my congregation.' So the young priest gets up and he wows them. He wows the Bishop, who looks around him and sees that the place is absolutely silent, and all of the people present there have wide open mouths and they're gazing in admiration at this priest. As the young priest speaks, he talks of love and duty and justice and all of those things, and he gets the message of Christianity across so well. When he comes down at the end, the Bishop walks over and tells him: 'That was extraordinary! That really is extraordinary! I've never seen anybody talk like that from a pulpit before. Quite, quite extraordinary! There's only one tiny piece of advice I would give you. When you're talking about the Holy

Trinity, please *don't* say: "Big Daddy, The Kid and Spooky".'

*

You get an Irish medical student doing the oral part of his final exams. The examiner holds up an object inside a glass container and asks: 'Now, what is that?' The student goes: 'Er, I think that's a knee cap.' The examiner says: 'It's a human brain!' Then he holds up another glass container: 'What is this?' The student goes: 'That, er, that's a . . . left foot!' The examiner replies: 'It is a skull!' The examiner holds up a third glass container: 'What is this?' The student goes: 'Ah, that's a jaw bone!' The examiner sighs: 'It is a leg!' He puts the container down: 'I find it rather remarkable that, after five years of studying medicine, you come in here and you know nothing at all!' The student says: 'Well, sir, I thought the exam was tomorrow!'

~

Paying to be Prudent

Banks. Banks used to promote this self-image: 'The Open Bank'; 'The Bank That Likes To Say *Yes!* Bank'. That's all gone now. Now the banks are: 'The Piss Off Bank'; 'The You're Out Of Your Mind Bank'; 'The Get Out Of Here You Arsehole Bank'; 'The We Don't Give A Shit Bank'. And banks charge you for everything now. You cash a cheque – they charge you. You buy a traveller's cheque – they charge you. You cash a traveller's cheque – they charge you. You ask for a phone call – they charge you. You ask for a reference – they charge you. You ask for financial advice – they charge you. And if you have £1 overdrawn – they will send you a reminder that costs you £25. And next week they will send you another reminder and it's £51. And if they send you one every week after that, at the end of the year you will owe these bastards £1,300. I say pay them by cheque.

~

Going For It

There's this little fella on a golf course in Ireland. He's just about to play off, and he's playing against a man whom he detests in life more than anybody or anything else. His whole ambition in life is to beat this man at golf. And he's just about to play off when: *phish-pop!* On to his shoulder: a leprechaun! The leprechaun looks at him and says: 'Would you like to get this hole in one?' The fella says: 'I would.' So the leprechaun says: 'Well, I'll tell you what: I'll sprinkle a bit of magic and you'll get that hole in one – provided that you promise to me that you will never covet or need or want a woman in your life. Will you give me that promise?' The fella says: 'Yes, I will.' So he puts the ball down: *boom!* A hole in one. *Eighteen* holes in eighteen. He not only beats the other fella, he *murders* him, and he's delighted. At the end of the game, the little leprechaun appears again – *phish-*

pop! – and says: 'You won't forget your promise?' The fella says: 'No, I won't.' The leprechaun reminds him: 'You'll never have anything to do with a woman in your life?' The fella assures him: 'I'll never have anything to do with a woman in my life.' So the leprechaun says: 'What's your name?' The fella says: 'O'Malley.' The leprechaun says: 'And what's your profession?' The fella says: 'I'm a Catholic priest.'

~

So To Sum Up . . .

In this world you have two things to worry about:
whether you are rich or whether you are poor.
If you are rich you have nothing to worry about.
If you are poor you have two things to worry about:
whether you are healthy, or whether you are sick.
If you are healthy you have nothing to worry about.
If you are sick you have two things to worry about:
whether you will live, or whether you will die.
If you live you have nothing to worry about.
If you die you have two things to worry about:
whether you go up, or whether you go down.
If you go up you have nothing to worry about.
If you go down, you will be so damn busy shaking
    hands with old friends,
you won't have time to worry.

~

4

Settling Down

Most people are other people.

Oscar Wilde

~

The theme of 'settling down' represented a classic Dave Allen dialectic. On the one hand, he – like the core of his audience during the days of Dave Allen At Large *– was settling down, or even already settled, in the sense of maintaining a career, a family, a reputation and a philosophy. On the other hand, he – again like so much of his audience – remained resistant to the notion of becoming 'set', like some sort of jelly, and fully assimilated into the image of middle age. Some of his routines, as a consequence, revolved around the various ways in which the sense of feeling settled can come as quite a relief: no more posing, no more pretence, no more wrong turns and false starts – one has earned an identity and carved out a niche for oneself in the world, and one can finally start to be far more open and honest and real. Some of his other routines, however, reflected on the fear of losing that youthful appetite for adventure, and that bright sense of rich possibility, once one submits to the routine and orderly world of acting like a responsible and respectable adult.*

He was good on the benefits to be had from being settled: the lowering of the guard, the opening-up of the personality and the arrival of sufficient courage to pursue one's truest convictions. There were routines about the revolutionary who had the cojones to win over a firing squad to his own political cause (and then order it to take aim on its old commander); the gay footballer who chose the occasion of a free kick by the opposing team to 'come out' (by cupping his hand around the cojones *of his next-door neighbour in the defensive wall); and there was the 'relaxed' Catholic who made love to his wife while a jazz trio played 'My Blue Heaven' beside the bed (prompting his partner to exclaim: 'Are you* sure *this is the rhythm method?').*

He was even better on the collapse into a life of quiet desperation: the reliance on the booze and the weed to block out the boredom; the switch from intense and unpredictable sex to routine and mechanical 'marital relations'; and the bleak and deep descent into the many empty rituals associated with the onset of middle age, such as organising and enduring the horrendously tense family Christmases, hosting a series of increasingly perfunctory 'cosy' dinner parties and planning some 'fun' annual excursions. The sketches on Dave Allen At Large *featured some memorable treatments of this theme, such as the one about the monks who become so frustrated at being stuck alongside each other inside the monastery that they break out into riots over the unfair distribution of their daily porridge; the one about the man who pursues his slightly younger lover across a deserted beach ('Yes, we* can!' *he assures her; 'No, we* can't!' *she insists) only to end up, after completing a trio of sandy trysts, desperate to escape from her clutches ('Yes,' she now insists, 'we* can!'; *'No,' he pleads with her tearfully, 'we* can't!'*); and the one about the little middle-aged man who is so impressed by his gadget-mad and upwardly-mobile friend's new hi-tech bachelor pad ('Everything* *works on a voice command') that he sits down in an easy chair and exclaims: 'Bugger me!' ('No!' screams his friend, but sadly a fraction belatedly).*

There is a veritable skinful of booze-related jokes in this section, simply because Dave Allen's drunks tended, more often than not, to be middle-aged drinkers who used alcohol as an emotional lubricant, or a catalyst for courage or just a routine glass-lined escape route. 'Drinking is basically social,' he once said, 'it's relaxation and it's generally fun and it allows you to drop your guard a little bit and be a bit more honest and open and be silly. I mean most of the gags, most of the boozy gags I've done, they're slightly innocent, and that's the way I like them to be.' His own on-screen alcoholic sidekick – in the glass that sat by his side – was there merely to wet the whistle: 'It really started basically when I was working in nightclubs,' he explained, 'and I'd be on stage and it was generally very hot and everybody else was kind of drinking around me so I used to bum an odd drink from some of the tables. I'd say, you know, "Can I have a glass of that?" or "Could I have a sip of that?" – just to cool down. And then I thought, "Well, no, I'll bring it on with me; I'll have my own – because then I don't have to drink what other people are drinking." And so that's basically where it started. On television, some people drink water or whatever, whereas I would drink just a little alcohol. Invariably it was champagne, because it's cool; whisky would make me hot.'

The jokes about smoking are here because of smoking's association, for Dave Allen's generation, with the trappings of established adulthood. He always claimed to have been *an early starter, taking his first 'quick drag' when he was about four or five as a misguided way of keeping up with his older brothers: 'My father believed in practical lessons, and he caught us smoking (not knowing that we were already hardened smokers) so he said he was going to teach us a lesson. He was a cigar smoker, and he used to roll them in cognac and then let them dry. He made us sit down with him and smoke one of these cigars each, so we sat there smoking while he waited for us to go green and yellow and vomit, and nothing happened.' The adult Allen gave the habit up, eventually, explaining: 'The cost had a lot to do with it: I got tired of paying others to kill me.'*

Most of the middle-aged characters in the comic material that follows puff and glug their way through life, doing their best to be 'normal'. The smoke usually obscures the stars, and the grog keeps out thoughts of the gutter, and most of them dream of something a little better, or imagine how things might be even worse. They are treated fairly kindly and are often let off quite lightly, because they live by rules flouted only by heroes or fools.

It was when Dave Allen was faced not with hope or despondency, but rather with the kind of contentment that bordered on smugness, that he was tempted to turn the ten-level comedy amp right up to level eleven and really give his victim a bit of a fright. When, for example, he was a guest on the Parkinson *chat show, he noted how smart the set design was compared to 'the old mat and a stool' that he had for his own humble show. 'I thought I should wear this suit tonight,' a smirking Michael Parkinson remarked, slouching back in his chair and wafting his legs in and out,* 'so that I might become anonymous and blend into the background.' Dave Allen looked him coolly in the eye, waited just a fraction of a second, and then replied: 'You don't have to wear the suit.'

G.M.

~

Grown-Up Uniformity

According to statisticians, middle-aged people are an incredibly predictable lot. The average adult person, we're told, will get married, have 1.8 babies, take 18,000 steps per day, travel 4,806 miles in their car per year, have sex 2.5 times a week, dream 121.6 dreams every month, blink 3,846,153 times each fortnight and fart fourteen times a day. It's a bit depressing if our lives get to be that predictable. It could be worse though. You could end up working as a statistician for a living.

~

Bad Habits

Drinking

Why do we drink alcohol? If you met somebody, say from outer space, who knew nothing about alcohol, and you said, 'Here, have a glass of booze,' he'd say, 'Why?' And you'd say, 'Well, drink it, taste it.' 'Ugh! Tastes awful!' So you'd say, 'Drink it.' 'But why?' You'd say, 'It'll make you feel good. It'll make you happy. Witty. Bright. Sharp.' 'Anything else?' You'd say, 'Yes. It'll make you sad. It makes you depressed. It makes you cry. It gives you headaches. Makes you bad-tempered. Makes you want to shoot your wife. Makes you miss. Gives you double vision. Shakes. Destroys your stomach lining. Kills your liver. Causes hardening of the arteries. And total destruction of the brain cells.' 'Then why do you drink it?' You'd say, 'For pleasure – what else?'

*

There are two drunks: one a very good fisherman, and the other has never fished in his life. And the second one says: 'Whaddle I do? Whaddle I do, to fish?' He said: 'Well, you get the hook . . . and-and-and you put bait on the hook.' And he does it. He says: 'Wh-Whaddle I do now?' 'You cast. Cast it out into da river.' And he goes *[Casts out into the river and then waits]*. He says: 'Whaddle I do now?' The other one says: 'Just wait. Jus-Just wait.' And after about twenty minutes he gets a bite: 'Wha-Wha-Whaddle I do now?' The other one says: 'Reel it in! Reel it in! Ree-Reel it in!' *[Starts reeling it in.]* And he reels it in so far that the fish is rammed up to the top of the rod! He says: 'Whaddle I do now?' The other one says: 'You climb to the top of the rod and you stab it to death!'

*

There are another two drunks walking down Piccadilly Circus, and, as they're walking, one of them drifts down into the Underground. And the other fella carries on walking into Leicester Square, until the first drunk comes right out again: 'Whe-Wh-Where you been?' The first drunk says: 'I-I dunno. I-I went down into some fella's cellar – he's got the biggest train set you've ever seen in yer life!'

*

You get the other fella walking down the road with a little penguin on a piece of string. The policeman says: 'Hey! Where did you get that penguin?' He said: 'I was-was walkin' down the road and-and it was there. Liddle penguin. And-and I saw him, and-and, s-saw him . . .' The policeman says: 'Well take him to the zoo.' So he says: 'O-O-Okay.' And off he goes. The next day the policeman is there, and, coming round the corner, is the drunk with the penguin. He says: 'I thought I told you to take that penguin to the zoo?' The fella says: 'I did. And it liked it. And-and I'm taking him to the library now!'

*

One drunk walks up to another fella and he says: 'Wha-What've you got in your sack? Wha-What is in that sack that you got there?' The other one says: 'He-Hed-Hedgehogs. I-I got hedgehogs in my sack.' The man says: 'How-How many hedgehogs have yer got in there?' The other one says: 'I-I'm not going to tell you.' The man says: 'If I can guess how many hedgehogs you got in your sack, will you give me one of them?' The other one says: 'Ha! I'll give you them both!'

*

Duck shooters. Two drunks, duck shooting in the hide, very early in the morning, very cold. No sign of the duck. So they have a little drop of rum to keep them warm. Still no sign of the duck. So they have another little drop. And still no sign of the duck. So they have another little drop, and-and-and another little drop. Then one big, fat, lonely, dirty duck goes across the sky, all by himself: *Quack-Quaaack! Quack-Quaaack!* And one of the drunks picks up his shotgun and goes: *Ba-Doom-Ba-Doom!* And the duck goes down into the lake. The other drunk's there and he says: 'That-that-that is what I call great shootin'!' His friend says: 'Well, you're bound to hit one out of a whole flock.'

*

A drunken man staggers into a Catholic church and sits down in a confession box, saying nothing. A minute or two passes. Not a word is spoken. The bewildered priest coughs to attract the man's attention, but still he says nothing. The priest then knocks on the wall – once, twice, three times – in a final attempt to get this man to speak. At long last, the drunk replies: 'It's no use knockin', mate, there's no paper in this one either.'

*

Each saint within the Catholic Church represents something. For example, St Peter is the patron saint of all fishermen; Christopher, before he got expelled, used to be for safety; and St Anthony is the saint that we pray to if we lose something. And there was this little drunken fella who's lost his wages, and he goes into the church and he prays. He's there by the statue of St Anthony and he says: 'St Anthony, O God love yer, I've lost the wages, and the children will starve all week, and-and the wife will belt me over the head! *Please*, St Anthony, if ye can help me: *help me to find me wages!!!* Er, I'll go off now and look for them.' And while he goes off, the woman who's cleaning the church bumps into the statue of St Anthony and knocks it over – smashes it to pieces. She goes: '*Eeeek! What have I done? WHAT HAVE I DONE?*' And the priest says: 'Don't worry, now, don't you fret yourself at all – we'll get another one. Just clear up the mess and, in the meantime, we'll put a little miniature statue there, so that people will know that St Anthony is still here.' So that's what they do: they put the little miniature there. And about half an hour later, the little drunken fella comes back, and he goes up to where the statue used to be and says: '*St Anthony?*' Then he looks down, sees the miniature and says to it: 'Will yer tell yer father that I found me wages?'

*

Two Irishmen go into a bar. One of them asks the bar-tender: 'Is there any good fishin' around here?' The bar-tender says: 'Do we have good fishin' here? Do we have good *fishin'* here! The fish are *thick* in the water! You don't even need to put the rod in! You just reach in and pull them out! Big salmon! [*Stretches his arms wide apart*] *THAT BIG!* I'll tell you what: when you're on your way home tonight, you get your friend there to hold you over the bridge by your legs and pull the salmon out of the water.' The two fellas agree: 'Yes, we'll try that when we get to the bridge!' So they get to the bridge, and one of them is held by his legs as he hangs upside down there for about three minutes, waiting for a salmon. All of a sudden, he shouts: *'PULL ME UP!'* His friend shouts back: 'Have you caught a salmon?' He says: 'No – *there's a train coming!'*

*

You get the drunk who arrives home and waiting for him is the very formidable figure of the wife, and she looks at him and she says: 'Drunk again?' He says: 'S-So am I.' She says: 'What does the clock say?' He says: 'The clock says, "Tock-Bong-Dingy-Ticky!"' She says: 'Where have you been?' He says: 'I-I've been with a-a sick friend.' She says: 'What's wrong with him?' He says: 'He's too sick to tell me.'

*

You get a little fella at a cocktail party. He goes up to the hostess and says: 'Ex-Ex-Excuse me, madam, but do-do lemons have feathers?' She says: 'I *beg* your pardon?' He says: 'D-Do lemons have feathers?' She says: 'I don't think so. Why?' He says: 'Oh, w-well, in that case I've just squeezed yer canary into my drink!'

*

We have in Ireland what we call 'the little people': leprechauns. There was a young fella walking along the beach, and, scuffling through the sand, he kicks what appears to be just the bottom of an old bottle. But as he kicks it, he disturbs all the sand around it, and sees that it's actually a very ancient bottle. So he pulls it out of the sand and he looks at it. There's a small piece of clear glass in it, and he looks through that, and finds that inside there is a leprechaun. And the leprechaun says: 'Let me out! *Please,* let me out! The wicked witch locked me in here 3,000 years ago and I've been here ever since! And I always told meself during the first thousand years that the first fella to let me out of here – I'd give him anything. And then I sat in here for another thousand years, and I thought that the first fella to let me out of here – I'd cut his legs off. And then I sat here for the third thousand years, and I said to meself that I'd grant the man who let me out three wishes – anything he wants!' So the fella says: 'Well, all right there, lad – I'll let you out!' *Pop!* Out comes the little leprechaun. He says: 'What do you want for your three wishes then? What do you want for your first wish?' The fella says: 'Well, it's hot, it's a very hot day today, and I've been walking round the beach for a long time – give us a large bottle of Guinness!' *Voom!* There it is. And he starts to drink it, and it's beautiful and cold and succulent. Lovely: *glug-glug-glug-glug!* Then the leprechaun says: 'Right: what will you be wanting for your other two wishes?' The fella, who now has lovely white foam all around his mouth, says: 'Now, you just wait a second! Wait just a second there! Don't hurry me! Just let me taste this! Let me *sample* it! Let me *enjoy* it!' So the leprechaun says: 'You can keep on drinking *that* forever! It's a special bottle: as soon as you've finished drinking it, it fills up again. It's one of *them* bottles!' The fella says: 'I don't believe it! I do not believe that!' So the leprechaun says: 'Well, go on then: try it.' So he does –

glug-glug-glug-glug – and the bottle goes totally empty, and then fills right back up again. And the fella says: 'My God! And I've still got *two* more wishes?' The leprechaun says: 'Yes.' So the fella says: 'I'll have two more of these!'

*

There's a fella who was staggering home with a pint of booze in his back pocket when he slipped and fell heavily. Struggling to his feet, he felt something wet running down his leg. 'Please, Lord,' he implored, 'let it be blood!'

*

A fella's got a bang on the nose. Top of the nose. He's in the pub, and everybody that he talks to, they all come up to him and say: 'What happened to your nose?' He says: 'I got banged on it.' Somebody else comes up and says: 'What happened to your nose?' He says: 'I got banged on it.' And after about eighteen times he's sick of it. Then someone else comes up and says: 'What happened to your nose?' He says: 'I *bit* it!' The person says: 'How the hell did you do that?' He says: *'I CLIMBED UP ON A CHAIR!'*

*

Two Irish fellas walk into a bar and ask for a drink. The barman says, 'Sorry, we're closed.' And one of the fellas says, 'How the hell did we get in, then?'

*

There are these two drunks in a bar. One of them – the drunker of the two – stands up and says: 'The Pope is a bum!' A big man on the other side of the bar walks over and looks at him menacingly: 'What did you say?' The drunk replies: 'I-I said that-that the Pope is a *bum!*' The big man pounds him hard and leaves him sprawled flat out on the floor. The drunk's friend rushes over and lifts him up: 'That was a *stupid* thing to say! Didn't you know that O'Reilly's a Catholic?' The drunk says: 'Sure I did – but I didn't know that the Pope was!'

*

There's one thing about drinking on television: people are fascinated to know what is in the glass. They're always asking me: 'What's in the glass? Is it whisky? Gin? Vodka? Rum? Brandy?' I always answer: 'Yes.'

~

Smoking

We smokers are what I would call the modern day leper. We are confined to 'areas'. We're not allowed to mix with the clean people. There used to be 'non-smoking compartments' on trains; now you have 'smoking compartments'. Two. Have you ever noticed where they are? One up the front, one down the back. Has anybody here ever heard of a train having an accident from the middle? 'He died, you know. He was a smoker.' 'Oh, smoking killed him?' 'No. He was sitting in the front of a train and it ran into a wall.'

I fly. People used to say: 'Have a nice flight.' Nowadays, the first thing they say is: 'Do you smoke?' 'Yes.' 'Smoking is confined to the area on the left-hand side of the plane.' And you go down there. You sit there, smoking. And there's a non-smoking area over there [*Points across the aisle*]. Two feet away from you. There's a fella sitting there, and he thinks that he's in a healthier area. And you're going:*Puff! Puff! Puff! Puff! Puff!*

I go to the cinema. The first thing they do when I go to the cinema: 'Do you smoke?' 'Yes.' 'The smoking area is on the right-hand side of the cinema.' And they put a *torch* on you. You're lit up, and the whole of the cinema's looking at you: 'Look at him! He's a dirty smoker! Urgh! Urgh!'

With all segregated areas, the only question is: 'Do you smoke?' They never ask you anything else. They don't ask you: 'Are you a Conservative? Are you Labour?' I mean, that can be as offensive to some people, but you don't get air hostesses going: 'Conservatives: over there on the right. Labour: on the left. Liberals: out on the wings – go on!' Nobody says: 'Are you Jewish? Catholic? Atheist?' Nobody says: 'Catholic? Conservative Catholic? *Two* Conservative Catholics? Put 'em together over there.' Nobody asks: 'Do you belch? Are you a belcher? Do you drink too much? Are you a bore?' 'Yes, I'm a bore.' 'Do we have another bore? Yes! Two bores. Put those two bloody bores together!' Nobody asks you *those* things!

~

Tics

A lot of people ask me why is it that, as I sit here, I am frequently seen brushing my trouser leg. And the answer is, because I drink my whiskey diluted. With vodka. And in the course of the evening I see the little fellas climbing up my trouser leg and what I'm doing is brushing them off.

And, uh, I went to see a psychiatrist about it, and I said: 'I have to keep brushing the little fellas off.'

And he said: 'Well, there's three things I want you to do. One is relax more, the second thing is to cut down on your drinking, and the third thing is to stop brushing the little perishers all over me!'

~

Sex

If you're not careful, you will find yourself going through the following three phases of sexual activity with your partner. The first phase is the 'everywhere' phase: you do it everywhere – in the car, in the yard, on the kitchen table, halfway up the stairs, everywhere. Then, after a little time passes, there's the 'bedroom' phase: things are settling down now, and the sexual activity rarely takes place anywhere except in the bedroom. And finally, there's the 'hallway' stage: you just pass each other in the hall and say, 'Screw you!'

~

Vibrators - increasing in size
phallic - objects

Russian - Image + reputation -

Women - approaching - Break ups in relationships -
I still want to be friends -
Serious talk -

Over development of wording (_American_)
ism - and ation - atitonic .

| Aunt Cissy - | School image |
| Father image | Tables - Alphabet - ! - |

Marriage

A woman goes to her parish priest and announces that she is going to be married. 'That's wonderful news,' says the priest. 'I hope you will both be very happy. Now what can I help you with?' She says: 'Well, I just have one question about marriage, Father, that I hope you might be able to answer for me.' A little nervously, wondering exactly what the question might be, the priest says: 'And what might that be?' The woman says: 'Well, Father, I'm not sure what colour dress I should wear for the wedding.' Somewhat relieved, the priest says: 'Oh, that's very simple. If you've been pure, you wear white, if not, you wear blue.' The woman smiles and says: 'Oh Father, thank you! I will wear white.' 'I'm delighted to hear it!' says the priest. And then she adds: 'With little blue spots.'

*

I think that it's rather unfair on priests that they're not allowed to get married. I really think that they *should* be allowed to get married. I think that if a priest meets another priest and they like one another they should be allowed to marry.

*

You get a priest and a nun, and the nun turns to the priest and she says: 'Do you ever think that the Holy Father will allow us members of the clergy to marry?' And he says: 'I don't think so, Mother Superior. Not in our lifetime. Or our children's. But perhaps in our children's children's.'

*

You get a man who goes to confession and he says: 'Father, I'd like to confess a sin. It's been a week since my last confession, and I had sex eight times last night with a woman.' The priest said: '*WHAT?*' He says: 'I had sex eight times last night with a woman.' The priest says: 'Who is this *harlot?*' The man says: 'My wife.' So the priest says: 'My son, having sex with your *wife* is a consummation of *marriage*. It's not a *sin*. Why are you telling me this?' The man says: 'Well, I just had to tell someone!'

*

There are two men, one quite young and the other middle-aged, sitting in the waiting room of a maternity hospital. The nervous younger man looks at the calmer older man and asks: 'How many children is this for you?' The older man says: 'Nine.' 'This is my first,' the younger man says. 'Yes,' says the older man, 'I can see that.' The young man shifts in his chair. 'Because you have had more experience, can I ask you a question?' The older man says, 'Go ahead.' 'I was wondering . . . well, you know . . . um, about how long after . . . ah, well, you know . . . can one have, um . . . you know, in bed.' The older man answers: 'Do you mean, how long after the birth can one make love again with one's wife?' The younger man stammers: 'Y-Y-Yes!' The older man says: 'Well, it depends.' 'Depends on what?' The older man says: 'It depends if your wife is in a ward or a private room.'

~

Procreation

Man creates, on average, four hundred million sperm per ejaculation. That struck me as extraordinary, because it only takes one little sperm to fertilise an egg. Why create so many? I met a gynaecologist friend of mine, and I asked him: 'Why, if it only takes one sperm, do we have four hundred million?' And he said: 'Because of the odds – to increase the odds of the sperm getting to the eggs. It's nature.' I said: 'Well, what do you mean?' He said: 'Well, because it's a tremendously difficult and arduous journey. Do you know that the sperm has as much chance of getting to the egg as you would have of swimming from the west of Ireland to America in super-glue? The sperm has got to fight all the way there.' And I said: 'Well, what happens to all the others?' He said: 'What do you mean, "What happens to them?" They're killed.' I said: 'They're *killed*? Who kills them?' He said: 'The defences of the female.' I said: 'Er, wait . . . wait . . .' He said: 'You've got to realise that the sperm is an outside force. It's an invader. So as soon as that invader enters the female it activates her defences and those defences come into operation to kill the sperm. What you've got to try and see in your mind is two gigantic armies at war.' So now, when I make love, that's how I think. And I'm coming to the conclusion that I must be the worst general in the world, because I've lost billions and billions of troops and I've only had a couple of victories! When I'm close to climax now I think: 'I don't want to lose another army. This is a volunteer force and they don't deserve to die so easily. I think I'll save 'em up for tomorrow, then I'll have eight hundred million and I'll really knock the other lot over!' But I do see it this way now. I see myself making love. I see my scrotum filling up with sperm, but I see it in my mind like Salisbury Plain and my army are all laid out – not like a modern-day army with khaki and guns, but like a medieval army with shields and breastplates, spears and bows and arrows – and there are legions of them, all with little tents laid out with flags fluttering. And I see General Sperm on a horse. The whole army is standing there, and he tells them: 'It's up to you. Stand still in the ranks – there'll be no premature ejaculation from this army!' I have heard myself, a split-second before I've climaxed, not say, 'I love you, darling!' or 'O God!' or 'Ooh-Ooh-Ooh!' I have heard myself shout into the darkness: '*CHAAAAAARGE!*' Four hundred million troops rush into the vagina: 'Where do we go? Where do we go? Where's the fallopian tube – head for the fallopian tube! Fallopian tube this way!' And suddenly: the alarms go off – *whoop-whoop-whoop* – and defenders appear from everywhere. 'I'll hold this lot back – you go that way! If I don't get through this, give this letter to my wife!' Can you imagine if the female is wearing spermicide? Troops running in there going: 'Aagh, spermicide! Spermicide masks: on!' Imagine if you're wearing a contraceptive: four hundred million troops charging into a rubber wall. *Bumph! Bumph! Bumph!* What you don't want is a courageous army. The battle would be over in a couple of seconds. You want a cowardly lot. Hanging back. What a sad end to an army it must be: gathered together at the end of a condom being dropped down the loo. 'Was that it?'

~

Parenthood

I always believed that I would never really become an 'adult' parent. I'd be a parent, but I'd understand. I'd sympathise with the younger generation. And then one day I was looking out the window, and I saw one of my children hit the other child very hard. *THUMP!* Right in the chest. And the little one went: '*Oooof!*' And all my instincts of fair play, my paternal instincts, kicked in and I ran out there and I went: 'What are you *doing?* What, what, what did you *do?*' The other child goes: 'He *hit* me!' So I say:

'Shut up, you! You keep out of it! *I'll* deal with this! Now: what did you do?'
'I hit him.'
'You *hit* him? You hit your brother?'
'Yes.'
'*Why?* Why did you hit him?'
'I don't like him!'

'You don't like him? You don't *like* him? So you go round *hitting* people because you don't *like* them? I don't like you!' *THUMP!* 'There: how do *you* like it, eh?' *THUMP!* 'How do you like *that*, eh?' *THUMP!* 'There's one thing you learn in life: you do not go through life hitting people who are smaller than yourself!' *THUMP!*

*

When your children get to be teenagers, they think that they can con you with money. And they do. 'Can I borrow a fiver?' Yeah. Two weeks later: 'Can I borrow a tenner?' But you owe me a fiver. 'Well, give me the tenner, and I'll give you a fiver.' Two weeks later: 'Can I have twenty?' But you owe me a tenner. 'Well, give me a twenty and I'll give you back ten.' It goes on to the point where my son will say to me: 'Can I have a hundred quid?' I'll say: 'No, you can't. I'm sick and tired of lending you money!' And he'll say to me: 'I always pay you back, don't I?'

~

Going with the Flow

Have you ever thought about what an extraordinary season Christmas is? Totally sane, normal people will rush off into the countryside and tear down holly trees, rip them asunder, grab great armfuls of ivy and climb to perilous heights to get a piece of mistletoe. For a month before Christmas the whole nation's walking around with trees under their arms. And nobody is surprised! I mean:

<u>DA/105 (F)</u>

<u>WAVE</u>

A DINING ROOM

A MAN IS SITTING AT A TABLE
EATING HIS BREAKFAST - READING
THE PAPER. A LITTLE SCHOOL GIRL
ENTERS.

GIRL:
Wave Daddy.

MAN WAVES

MAN:
Bye.

GIRL:
(MORE URGENTLY) Wave.

MAN:
(WAVING FURIOUSLY) Goodbye.

GIRL:
(DESPERATE) No. Wave!

A DOOR BEHIND THE MAN BURSTS
OPEN AND AN ENORMOUS AMOUNT OF
WATER ENGULFS HIM.

what for? When you think about it: we bring a twelve-foot tree into our sitting-room! To decorate it. And the whole family sits there going: 'Oh, that tree looks lovely!' Try doing it in July: 'What's that bloody tree doing in here?'

How does a custom like Christmas trees even begin? Some fella walking around with a tree, and someone goes: 'Where are you going with the tree?' And he says: 'I'm takin' it home.' 'What are you going to do – burn it?' The fella says: 'Nope. I'm going put it in the room.' 'You are?' He says: 'Yeah. And then I'm going to cover it in tinsel and lots of little glass balls, chocolate figures, and I have this brilliant idea of putting a fairy right at the top!' And nobody says: 'You're a bloody lunatic!' They all said: 'That's a great idea! Let me do it!'

Turkeys. Eleven months of the year we wouldn't dream of eating turkeys. Come Christmas, we all run around going: 'Where's the turkey? Gotta have a turkey! Christmas wouldn't be Christmas without a turkey!' Mind you, it's just as well that we eat turkeys, because otherwise the world would be up to its bum in them.

And cards. We all send each other Christmas cards. You know the screwiest Christmas card I got this year? It wishes me peace and prosperity, and comes from Bomber Command . . .

And music. All of the Christmas music is so *noisy*. It's: 'The church bells are *ringing!*'; 'Church bells at even-tide!'; 'Jingle bells, Jingle bells!'; 'Sleigh bells!'; 'Hear the angel trumpet sound!'; 'Hark the herald angels sing!'; 'Shout "Hallelujah" ye choirs of Heaven!'; 'Ding-Dong merrily on high!'; 'Blow, trumpeter, the babe is born!'

You'd think with all of that noise going on when he was being born, those three wise men wouldn't have needed a star! 'Listen. . . . Aha! *That's* where he is – forget about the star, let's go!' And when you hear the little drummer boy, with his little drum: '*Drrrrrrum! Drrrrrruum! Drrrrrruuum!*' Can you see the Virgin in the stable: all the din from Heaven – the choirs and the trumpets and the heavenly bells – has stopped, and she's just got her newborn babe to sleep . . . and who comes marching up the road? '*Drrrrrrum! Drrrrrruum! Drrrrrruuum! SHALL I PLAY TO HIM RUM PUM PUM UPON MY DRUM? Drrrrrrum! Drrrrrruum! –*' '*NOOOOO! JOSEPH – TELL THAT KID TO STICK THAT DRUM UP HIS BUM!!!*'

~

Embracing Our Imperfection

There is a word in the English language which is called a 'malaprop'. It was created by an Irish writer called Sheridan in a play called *The Rivals*. It's the tendency to mix up your words, to confuse similar sounding words and use them out of context. It's like saying: 'I'm living on subsidence.' Or: 'I can't see through the window because of the compensation.' I've actually heard male Jewish children say they've had an operation on their 'gentiles'. A woman could not have a child because she was 'impregnable', 'inconceivable' or 'unbearable'. I saw a fella in court in Dublin, standing in the dock, and he had both his hands in his trouser pockets and he was chewing gum very noisily right throughout the whole proceedings. *Smack-Smack-Smack-Smack!* Eventually, the judge says: 'Young man, would you kindly stop masticating?' And the fella said: 'I'm sorry, my lord!' Then he took his hands out of his pockets. I saw another man who'd been charged with some sort of sexual offence, and he was swearing, under oath, that he could not have committed the said sexual offence because, at the time of that said sexual offence, he was suffering from the dreaded 'Venetian Disease'. And his counsel stood up and said: 'My Lord, I think my client meant to say he had a touch of the gondoliers.'

*

I suppose another man who has made his humorous mark on the English language is the Reverend William Spooner. Because of him, the term 'Spoonerism' was created. It's sort of getting your words all mixed up, something we've all done. It makes you smile. For example, instead of a 'carked par', you get – I've just done it! You get a 'cuff of coppee'. A 'glass of moe with kilk'. You wait for a number thirty-nine at the 'stus bop' and you're 'under the alfulence of incohol'. At Christmas we always 'goosed the cook'. There's 'many a rude turd spoken in jest'.

I don't know why it happens. Just the other day I heard myself do it. We have here something called the outside broadcasting cameras and I called them the 'outcast broadsiding cameras'.

When I was in school, I was described as a 'mick in the

stud'. I said, 'Don't you mean "stick in the mud"?', and they said, 'I don't know me what I teen.'

I heard an Australian politician describe the immigrant population crisis as the 'eminent copulation crisis'. I heard David Steel, the former Liberal leader, described as a 'fart young smeller'.

Many years ago, I was listening to the BBC Home Service, and what I was listening to was called 'Folk Songs from Poland'. Exactly. The announcer came on and he said: 'Ladies and gentlemen, you've just been listening to Six Polk Songs from Foland.'

And I heard a fella on the radio in Ireland. Burl Ives, the old American folk singer, was in Ireland a while ago, and I heard this fella, one of the local DJs, on the radio say: 'Burl Ives is over here making a film, and there's been lots of requests for one of Burl Ives' songs, one of his big hits, "The Big Rock Candy Mountain".' So they played it. And then the fella comes back and he says: 'Well, that was Burl Ives singing "The Big Cock Randy Mountain".' There were cars all over Ireland disappearing into hedges!

~

5

Mid-Life Crises

I call on those that call me son,
Grandson, or great-grandson,
On uncles, aunts, great-uncles or great-aunts,
To judge what I have done.
Have I, that put it into words,
Spoilt what old loins have sent?
Eyes spiritualised by death can judge,
I cannot, but I am not content.

William Butler Yeats

~

The mid-life crisis has never been really uncommon, but, during the era of Dave Allen At Large, *it had come close to seeming obligatory. In 1974, for example, the 39-year-old Richard Bingham, the Seventh Earl of Lucan, slipped off into the night following a murder at his family's London home in Lower Belgrave Street; and during the same year, the 49-year-old Labour MP and former Postmaster General John Stonehouse faked his suicide by leaving his clothes on a Miami beach, and then fled to Australia in disguise and on a false passport with the intention of setting up a new life for himself with his former secretary Sheila Buckley, a 28-year-old divorcee (he was eventually tracked down and jailed for seven years for theft and false pretences). In 1976,* The Fall and Rise of Reginald Perrin *– a sitcom about a 46-year-old desk-bound sales executive who, in a last-ditch attempt to preserve his sanity and escape the rat-race, fakes his own death and walks off into the sunset – was screened on BBC1. That year also saw the opening of the Hollywood movie* Network, *in which a middle-aged newscaster called Howard Beale (played by Peter Finch) cracks up on air, rages about the horrible state of the world in general and television in particular, and concludes his tirade by ordering his viewers to 'Go to the window and shout as loud as* you can: "I'm mad as hell and I'm not going to take it any more!"'

Dave Allen joked about them all. Referring in 1976, for example, to the reports concerning the threatened loss of some of Britain's best brains in the so-called 'brain drain', he pointed out that only one politician had left the country during the last decade, and 'they brought him back and gave him seven years!' He remained intrigued, however, by the idea, as well as the phenomenon, of ordinary people reaching middle age and then suddenly bidding to drop out and dodge their destiny.

He even played a man in the midst of a mid-life crisis himself when, in 1979, he gave a tender and moving performance in Alan Bennett's television play One Fine Day as George Phillips, a kindly but ineffectual estate agent (described by Bennett as 'the writer in disguise') whose low-key personality renders him practically invisible at work and at home. Appalled by the kind of cut-throat tactics employed by most of his colleagues and acutely allergic to their jargon-filled conversations, George takes refuge surreptitiously in a large high-rise office building in north London that he is meant to be renting to his company's clients. Relaxing in solitude on the roof, he listens to music through his headphones and drifts off into his own little private world. This reverie is rudely ended when a security guard locks the hatch that he used to gain access, and he finds that the only way he can escape is to smash a window pane on the top floor. George is oddly exhilarated by this experience, and returns to his old life a changed man – his own man.

There were similar little epiphanies in some of his sketches, but more often than not the characters were subjected to yet another comical slap in the face. There was the middle-aged motorist who became so frustrated by the lack of parking spaces for anyone other than the disabled that he proceeds to saw one of his legs off – and while he does so another able-bodied motorist drives straight into the only free place available. There was the sober-suited businessman who managed to slip away for an intimate candle-lit dinner with his new young girlfriend. 'Do you know, my darling,' he remarks dreamily, 'in this light you don't look a day over fourteen.' 'I'm not,' she replies casually, as he chokes on his Chardonnay. Then there was the married man whose cuddle in the bed of his lover ended abruptly when she heard a car and cried out: 'Oh, my God, it's my husband – hide!' After ten seconds or so of cowering in the closet, he reappears, looking confused, and exclaims: 'Wait a moment: I'm your husband! We need to talk!' 'Yes,' replies his wife angrily, 'we do!'

One classic Dave Allen At Large *sketch epitomised his appreciation of the horrors to be had from ending up stuck in a dead-end job. One man – flat cap dozing on his hang-down head, fag drooping over his chin, hands stuffed away inside his pockets, scuffed shoes shuffling reluctantly ahead – makes his way down a grey-slabbed street one drab-looking weekday morning; he is soon joined by another, similarly tired and attired, working man ('Mornin''; 'Mornin'') who follows him closely in a slow but synchronised shuffle; then two more tag along, equally close and similarly synchronised ('Mornin''; 'Mornin''); then* another two ('Mornin''; 'Mornin''); then another two ('Mornin''; 'Mornin''); and so it goes on, street after street, corner after corner, with all of them jammed up close but impersonal like a line of Lowry men doing the conga under extreme duress. Eventually, they all trudge through the same pair of factory gates, and we see the sign: 'PRESTIGE SARDINE PACKING COMPANY'.

Similarly, another clever little sketch reflected on the horrors to be had from ending up stuck without even the discomfort of a dead-end job: a man at the front of a long queue is called inside a cold, grey and miserable-looking building; a sign saying 'UNEMPLOYED THIS WAY' points him up a flight of stairs, and then up another flight of stairs; the next sign sends him along a long corridor; the next one directs him along another, even longer, corridor; he then goes through a door and finds a sign that guides him through another door, and then down another long corridor; a sign at the end of that sends him down a flight of stairs; and then down another flight of stairs; then a sign – 'UNEMPLOYED THIS WAY' – invites him to push open a door; so he does, and finds himself back outside – right at the end of the same queue he had recently left at the front. No wonder, the implication was, that even decent people sometimes dream of disappearing and lying doggo for a while.

Dave Allen was also a fan of those who dared, at a relatively mature stage in their lives, to start being different. He agreed completely with the dictum of John Stuart Mill: 'In this age the mere example of non-conformity, the mere refusal to bend the knee to custom, is itself a service.' Unusually for someone who had found a niche for himself within the world of mainstream entertainment, Dave Allen remained an avid champion of eccentrics and rebels and active existentialists; he sympathised with their refusal, or inability, to march along to the mechanical beat of the modern drum. During the course of making his fascinating 1970s documentaries, Dave Allen in Search of Great British Eccentrics *and* Dave Allen and Friends, *he tracked down a rich and colourful range of contemporary non-conformists, including the man who had built himself a huge stone pineapple in his garden – large enough for him to live in – simply because he had always been especially fond of that particular fruit; he also encountered a country vicar who liked to dress up as a cowboy; a group of extreme cheese-rollers in Gloucestershire; and a couple who ran their elaborate model railway entirely and indefinitely in strict accordance with the 1938 timetable out of St Pancras. 'It's all about individuality of one kind or another,' he explained. 'I wanted to film people who were resolutely doing their own thing – not loonies or even eccentrics necessarily, just people who passionately believed in doing something that very few others would ever think of doing.' He reflected: 'There's an inner contentment about people like that which makes me think that we're the eccentric ones – sitting in airport traffic jams, getting into planes, spending six hours in the air just to get into another traffic jam in New York behind a cab driver who blows his horn and charges you money for sitting there with him. What's sane about that?'*

Lesser comedians – especially the ones who were afforded plenty of airtime during the era of the 1970s and

80s – often mocked people purely on account of them being different. Dave Allen never did. That was one of the things that made him so admirably different.

G.M.

~

There's quite a famous story about my father. He was with the *Irish Times*, and the editor of the time was a fella called Smyllie, who was a very well-known Irish journalist, and one of their columnists was Myles na Gopaleen, who was also known as Flann O'Brien. And the three of them had put the paper to bed one night and then they had gone off to have a drink. At that time in Ireland, the pubs where you could drink late at night were called 'bona fide pubs' – that meant you had to travel a certain distance, and be a 'bona fide traveller', to enter the pub. So my father, Smyllie and Myles got a cab and drove to a pub about three miles out – somewhere around Rathdown, which is County Dublin – and they got out of the cab, knocked on the door of the pub, as you had to do, and then they were let inside. So they were in there for about three or four minutes, and they're having their drinks, and then Smyllie says: 'That fella over there by the bar – I've seen him. I've seen him somewhere before. Where have I seen him? Don't know, don't know . . .' He feels a bit uneasy. So they decide that they'll go off somewhere else for the next drink. So they go out, get in the cab, go off and arrive at another pub. And then about five minutes later, the same fella who'd been in the first pub comes into the second pub. Now, at the time, my father was under the threat of being shot for some or other political reason. I honestly don't know what it was, but my father used to say things to us like, 'Don't let strangers come and ask you things. Don't answer them when they ask you what time your dad comes home or what time he goes out or anything like that.' But I learnt years later that he'd been threatened with execution. And so, when he sees this strange man by the bar, his immediate thought is: 'This fella's following me.' So they go out again, get in the cab and drive off to another pub. And they're sitting in there, having a drink, when, sure enough, the same fella arrives. And my father had a very, very quick temper, in the sense that it was there one moment and gone the next, so he just put down his drink, strode over and punched this fella. Now he's in a terrible rage. He's sitting on the man's chest, he's got the man's head in his hands and he's banging it on and off the ground, saying: '*You filthy, sly, little fucking gun man bastard! Think you could fucking shoot me in the back, you bastard? What are you following me for?*' And the fella says: 'I'm your cab driver.'

~

Quiet Desperation

There was an unfortunate man who, throughout his life, kept on finding himself in the position where he had to choose between two options, and he always chose the wrong one. He had the choice between two universities, Oxford and Cambridge, and he picked Oxford. He had to choose between two degrees, and he picked the wrong one for his particular talents. He had to choose between two jobs, and his choice turned out to be the one with the least chance of advancement. He had to choose between two women to marry, and he picked the one who ended up as the nag. And finally, after twenty years, he decided that he had had enough and he would get away and start all over. So he boards a jet at Heathrow and sets off on what he hopes will be a life-changing trip. Midway through the flight, however, the pilot reports that they have lost engines 2, 3 and 4, and that the last one is likely to go very soon. So the man looks to Heaven and cries out: 'St Francis, help me!' A voice comes from above: 'Would that be St Francis Xavier or St Francis of Assisi?'

~

Tense Nervous Headaches

We're under pressure. I started to read up about stress. Stress basically is what your body creates. For example, it's energy, a mixture of your brain creating with chemicals energy for your body either to run from or fight whatever it is that's causing you anxiety. It goes back to early man where a caveman would come around and see a tiger and he would immediately go into stress. Great oceans of energy would suddenly be in your system. You'd either run away or pick up a rock and brain the bastard.

In our society you can see how certain people, and certain situations, put you under stress. Your boss might say: 'Is it possible to have a word with you?' When the boss says that, your body is immediately in stress, but instead of picking up a chair and braining the bastard you sit there and get into more and more stress.

You see people with cars who are subjected to the most extraordinary stress. It happens to me. As soon as I get behind the wheel of a car, I'm like anybody else: a bastard. I'm sure everybody's the same: no man is a man anymore, he's not a chap or a fellow, he's a bastard – a hairy bastard, a fat bastard, a thin bastard, a small bastard or a big bastard, but definitely a bastard. I mean, if I'm walking up the street, I'm not worried about space. I don't want to overtake people when I'm on the pavement. I don't try to cut people up. But when I get behind the wheel of a car I'm possessive; I'll run the bastard down if he gets between me and another car. It's this terrible anger that gets created.

~

Glimpsing the Infinite Regress

If you were to wake up one morning and you knew everything that the day held for you – exactly what was going to happen, who you were going to meet, what you were going to say, what you were going to eat . . . – you would not get out of bed. You'd just stay there . . . and then all those things that were going to happen, wouldn't happen. Therefore, you would have known that you weren't going to get out of bed. And if you'd known *that*, you wouldn't have thought about all those things that weren't going to happen anyhow.

*

"Labour, work, study, if you want to earn",
His parents admonished in voices stern.
Don't sit and dream, apply your mind
To matters of a more important kind
To search for happiness is not a joy.
Did you hear what I said you stupid boy
"Work, work, work, if you want to get ahead"
So he bought himself a length of rope
And topped himself instead.

DA.

Claustrophobia

Christmas, especially, is a stressful time of the year for families. Watch yourself over the Christmas period: your family become enemies. Everybody needs wiping out. Your smile tightens. Your voice – which used to be cheery: 'Ho-Ho-Ho!' – is now angry: '*No you can't! Put it down! Stop it! If anybody else does that again, by Christ, I'll smack 'em! MY GOD! – WE'RE MEANT TO BE HAVING A GOOD TIME!!!'*

*

When you think about what is 'bad' for us, or what the Government thinks is bad for us – smoking, drinking, excessive eating – now, in years to come, they're going to start worrying about the population explosion. There's too many people. But they won't tell you not to screw, because that would get them out of office. But they'll start telling you little things like: 'Are you aware of the pressure that the heart is under during the climax of the act of love?' They're already starting. I read the other day that it is far safer for a man to have sex with his wife than his mistress. And people will start to think about it. I honestly believe, in years to come, when you buy a contraceptive it will have a health warning on it: 'HER MAJESTY'S GOVERNMENT WISHES TO INFORM YOU THAT SEX CAN BE DANGEROUS TO YOUR HEALTH'. Written in little letters in the rubber. And you'll watch that warning grow before your eyes.

~

Anti-Social Behaviour

The English sense of humour is subtle, and tinged with sarcasm. For example, you get the two English gentlemen talking to one another, and one of them says: 'I passed your house yesterday.' So the other one says: 'Thank you.'

*

A man finds a bottle washed up along the shore, and inside it is a leprechaun. The man knows that the leprechaun would vanish if he took his eyes off it, but the leprechaun explains that he is not a 'crock o' gold' leprechaun, but rather a 'three wish' leprechaun. And besides, the leprechaun adds, everything that the man wishes for, he is bound to give double to his mortal enemy – whom the leprechaun happens to know is old Tom O'Flaherty. The man agrees. 'So what is your first wish?' asks the leprechaun. The man says, 'I want a twenty-five-room house.' And, sure enough, a twenty-five-room house pops up – and O'Flaherty suddenly finds himself sitting on the porch of a *fifty*-room house, saying, 'God love ya!' and all of that. 'What now is your second wish?' asks the leprechaun. The man says, 'I want twenty of the most beautiful girls in all of the world.' And, sure enough, twenty gorgeous-looking girls are with him on his porch, and, all of a sudden, O'Flaherty has *forty* on his, saying, 'Oh, bless ya!' and 'I didn't know you cared!' and all that. Then the leprechaun says, 'What is your third and last wish?' The man says, 'I wish that my desire for women be cut by fifty per cent . . .'

Diets

Years ago, people used to enjoy food. People would say: 'Eat your food – it's good for you.' Nowadays, food has somehow become 'unhealthy'. It's bad for you. It has things in it like 'cholesterol' and 'carbohydrates' – words we'd never heard of. And all the time, at the back of the mind, there's a part of you thinking: 'Oh, I'd *love* to eat that food!' The other part is saying: 'No! You *can't* eat it! *Mustn't eat it!*' And they go to bed at night, and they don't have good, Freudian dreams about snakes, spiders and sharks. They dream about apple pies, covered in cream, with legs, dancing and saying: '*Eat meeeeee – I am luverleeee!*' They have nightmares. They wake up screaming: '*Eeaaghh!* I had another nightmare about that apple pie!'

Everywhere you go nowadays people are talking about losing weight: 'I lost four pounds.' 'I lost three pounds.' 'I lost eight pounds.' '*I* lost sixteen pounds!' 'I read about a woman the other day who lost eighteen *stone!*' Now, one of the first lessons I ever learned regarding mathematics is that matter is matter. It can change its shape but it doesn't go anywhere. So every time I hear all of these people saying, 'I lost this much' and 'I lost that much', I think: 'Where is all this fat? Where *is* it? Where do they *keep* it? Is it in a drawer upstairs? "This is my fat drawer – I keep all of my fat in it, see: *wobble-wobble-wobble*". What's in the cupboard? "Don't go in there! That's where all of my *fat* is!" Maybe it's in black plastic bags underneath the stairs. Every Wednesday at three o'clock in the morning: *Knock-knock!* "Who's there?" *[Whispers]* "We're the Fat Collectors".'

And then I think to myself: 'No, hang on a second. It can't be. Because every time I hear somebody say, "I've lost three pounds," I hear somebody else say, "I've put *on* three pounds".' Then I think to myself: 'It's just the one lump of fat that's going through humanity!'

*

I'm quite convinced that, probably in about ten or twenty years' time, when you buy food it will have a health warning on it: *'FOOD IS DANGEROUS TO YOUR HEALTH'*.

*

It seems like the only way to have a healthy life these days is not to eat. Starve to death – at least when you're dying you'll know you're not dying of anything serious!

Discontentment

When you're young, you keep asking people what things are, and why they are. When you reach middle age, young people start asking *you* what things are, and why they are. And it's at that point that you realise that the people who told you what things are, and why they are, didn't really know what they were talking about, and you don't know what you're talking about either. So that's when you start telling other people to shut up.

~

Sexual Disorientation

Women are much more independent now, and I'm very pleased to see it. They're much more aware of their own sex. They're not quite so prepared to play that subservient role to the hairy macho that existed. I mean, there was a time when girls would wait for the initial advance from the male – which generally came after the pubs had closed, and, in between Technicolor yawns and belches, her body was subjected to a kind of groping and fumbling attack. Now there's a reversal, a role reversal, taking place. Women are much more prepared to go out and, if they fancy some fella, they're not going to sit on the other side of the room and wait for some kind of magical thing to happen – a woman's quite prepared to go across and pick up the fella. Pass a compliment, tell him he looks nice – 'You've got nice clothes'; 'I like your hair' – she might even give him a sudden grope. So I've heard. And nowadays they're much more direct about sex, and what sex is for them, and quite rightly. I mean, women will talk about orgasms: 'It's my *right* to have an orgasm! I'm not your sexual plaything! I *want!* I want – you had it last night, it's my turn tonight!'

But the *male* now doesn't know how to react to this.

He was the hunter. Now he's the hunted! He doesn't know why: he can't do the foreplay, he doesn't know what to do with it. She's telling him: 'I want an orgasm – and I'd *prefer* it if we could have one together! Do you think you might be able to manage that?' The male, he doesn't know what to *do*. He retreats. Women are now the ones saying: 'Are we going to make love or are you just going to lie there?' And the man will try saying things like: 'Er, oh, I, um, I haven't taken any precautions.' The woman goes: 'That's all right – I took the pill an hour ago. Come on, get on with it!' He'll say things he's never said before, like: 'I'm getting a headache, I think . . .' And she'll say: 'Ha! I've got something to cure that! *Grrrr!*'

There is a total turnabout now in male and female sexual relationships. The *male* is actually faking the orgasm! He's lying there now going [*Weakly*]: 'Ha-a-ah-hu-hurrrrr . . .' He doesn't know how to react. Because he's under pressure like this, the male doesn't know what to *do*, so he gets *nervous*, and because of that he gets *tense*. The whole thing about *pleasurable* sex is to do it in a totally relaxed and open state. But this is: 'Come *on!*' 'Er, right . . .' Inside he's thinking: 'I hope it's good! I-I hope she *likes* it! I-I-I hope it comes *up!* If it does come up I hope it doesn't go *down* again! Oh, *no* – I hope I'm not going to have one of those premature ejaculations! *Doh!* I-I'm sorry, darling, this never happened before!' '*Ah, shaddup!*'

185

DA/59 (S)

BREADSTICKS.

RESTAURANT.

ROMANTIC ATMOSPHERE — ONE SIDE
OF THE RESTAURANT THERE IS A
MAN DINING ALONE. HE NOTICES
OVER THE OTHER SIDE A PRETTY
GIRL — ALSO DINING ALONE.
SHE PICKS UP A STICK OF BREAD
AND PLACES IT AGAINST HER LIPS.
HE WATCHES WITH INTEREST.
SHE NIBBLES THE END. HE WATCHES
WITH MORE INTEREST.

SHE STARTS TO LICK THE BREADSTICK
FROM HALF WAY UP TO THE END.
HE GETS EXCITED.

HER TONGUE EXPLORES AROUND THE
BREADSTICK. SHE SEEMS ABOUT
TO TAKE IT ALL IN. HE GETS
POSITIVELY OVER-EXCITED.
SHE BITES THROUGH IT WITH A
SCRUNCH. HE REACTS IN AGONY...

Sexual Addiction

PRIEST: D'you have a confession to make, my son?
MAN: Yes, Father, I am a sinner.
PRIEST: Ah, well, we all are.
MAN: Father, I have indulged in pleasures of the flesh. My every waking moment is spent with a woman. Any woman. All day, all night. I just can't help myself.
PRIEST: Well, all you can do is pray for strength.

~

Cracked Marriages

There's a curious statistic I came across recently. The average married couple converse for twenty minutes every week. What do they find to talk about?

*

I suppose the greatest example of the unexpected is the man who knows that his wife is having an affair with the milkman, and goes home expecting to find his wife in bed with the said milkman. But it's not. It's the baker. In bed with the milkman.

*

You get a young lady at home. There's a knock on the door. She opens it and there's a fella standing there who says: 'Mary, your husband asked me to pop in to tell you he's working late in the office. He'll not be home for two hours.' She says: 'Oh, that's very nice of you. Will you come in and have a cup of tea?' He says: 'I will indeed.' So they're having a cup of tea, and he's looking at her and he says: 'You know, Mary, I've always fancied you. I've always had the picture in me head of my arms circling around your minute little waist, your soft voluptuous lips close to mine, and I see a picture in me head of you and I *darting* upstairs together and committing one of them deadly mortal sins!' She says: 'What about my husband?' The fella says: 'He won't be back for two hours. And besides that, if you and I go upstairs together, I have in me pocket three hundred and fifteen pounds and fifteen pence!' She says: 'For me? Three hundred and fifteen pounds and fifteen pence? If we go upstairs together?' *Va-voom!* They're up there. It happens, he leaves, and two hours later the husband comes back and she says: 'Your friend popped in to tell me you were working late.' He says: 'Never mind that – did he give you me wages?'

*

A husband opens his hotel room and discovers his wife in bed with her arms around another man. 'What are you doing in bed with my wife?' he exclaims. The other man looks at him, looks at the woman, looks back at him and then back at the woman. 'You're right,' the man says to the woman. 'He *is* stupid!'

*

A drunk finds out that his wife is having an affair, so he confronts her: 'I-I have heard about your infidelity.

[Sob!] You-you've betrayed me! [Sob!] I'm-I'm going to put an end to it all!' He takes out a revolver, loads it, and puts it to his head. His wife just sits in the corner laughing. 'Don't laugh,' he says. 'You're next!'

*

In Venice, there's a gondolier who tells his wife: 'I'm-a sick and-a tired of you! I'm-a going away!' His wife cries: 'But-But what about the little bambini?' The man shouts: 'You can have-a them!' The wife cries out: 'But what about my spaghetti?'

He shouts back: 'I don't-a want-a your spaghetti, or your lasagne, or your *fettuccini!*'

So she cries: 'But what about-a last night, when we lay together in bed?' The man turns and says: 'You know, one of these days I'm gonna go! I don't know when it's gonna be, but one of these days.'

*

This past Christmas, my wife gave me two neckties. I got up Christmas morning, put one of them on, went downstairs, showed it to her, and the first thing that she said was: 'And just what was wrong with the other one?'

*

There was once a man who had over ten children. He said that if his wife ever had another one, he'd hang himself. Nine months later, she had another child. 'Are you going to hang yourself?' the wife asked. 'No,' he says, 'I'll give myself a reprieve. But if it happens again, I am hanging myself!' Nine months later, she has yet another child. The husband says, 'Right, that's it!' He goes off, gets the rope, pulls out the chair and stands on it. He's just about to put the rope over the beam when he hears from his wife: 'Just a moment: you might be hanging the wrong man!'

*

Picture the scene: a timid-looking, plainly-dressed middle-aged man – his short hair well-oiled and sharply-parted, his small wire glasses picked out by a solitary shaft of light – stands in the middle of some dark and echoing room . . .

My Lord, may I speak to the ladies and gentlemen of the jury before they leave to reach the verdict, and before you, my Lord, pass sentence upon that verdict? Thank you. You have heard that for many years I lived a happy and simple bachelor existence. And, like most bachelors, I was rather set in my ways. I was an active member of the local church society. I also belonged to a small music appreciation group, made up of some very close friends. It was during one of these musical evenings that I first met the woman who was later to become my wife. She was actually everything that a man could have wished for: she was attractive and witty and intelligent, but, above all, she shared – or at least she gave the appearance of sharing – my interests. It was only in the following months that I began to see her as she really was. She created such embarrassing scenes that gradually, one by one, my friends began to stay away. I had to suffer her sulks, her fits of frenzied rage, her long accusing silences. Until eventually she just followed me about the house, *nagging* incessantly. There was no escape from her *shrewish* voice. And then, on the night referred to by the Prosecution, she followed me down to the last sanctuary that I had: the cellar. My mind snapped. I could take no more. I picked up a hammer, and, as she turned to face me, mocking laughter fell from her twisted mouth. There was no fear in her eyes. She dared me to hit her – she actually *dared* me – and, God forgive me, I did. I struck again, and again, and *again*.

[*A woman's voice calls out: 'Henry!'*]

Yes, dear?

[*'What are you doing down there in the cellar?*]

Just practising. Just practising . . .

~

Damaged Ideals

Personal

After a while you stop worrying so much about whether the glass is half full or half empty. You start being more concerned about how big the glass is.

~

Religious

As you've probably gathered, I was educated by the Catholic clergy. God's storm troopers. One of the things that I've never understood about the Catholic religion is the inequality between the sexes. I mean, as far as a woman is concerned, all she can do, the most top job that she can get, is Mother Superior. That's as far as she can go. Men, on the other hand, can become priests, then monsignors, bishops, archbishops, cardinals . . . they keep on going up . . . and, finally, the Pope. The other thing I've never understood about this religion is that the higher up you go in rank, the better your clothes get. I mean, the priests – the little, lowly priests – they're all drab, they're all in black. Move up to the monsignors and you get a little bit of colour – magenta. Then the bishops: they can wear black and they can wear purple, and they can wear black with red trimmings. The archbishops: they can wear black and purple. The cardinals: bright red! And the Pope: he can wear anything – he's got white, yellow, black, purple . . . he can wear rings, jewellery, little hats, big hats, *enormous* hats. Can you imagine him opening his wardrobe each morning: 'Hmmmmmmm, well, what shall I wear today?'

*

By the way, did you see that this latest Pope – the Polish Pope – has just been down to Australia? The trip was sponsored by a *brewery!* What next – Durex?

*

The only way that you could bring me back into the Catholic Church is to have a Chinese Pope. I would love a Chinese Pope to be elected. Can you imagine receiving

Holy Communion from a Chinese Pope? You'd kneel down and he'd go: 'Ah, you going to have this here, or take away?'

*

Four priests were aboard a train heading from Edinburgh to London for a conference. Since they were all by themselves inside their travelling car, they decided to convey their secret vices to one another. 'We're all men of God,' one of them says, 'so let's be totally honest with each other.' And they all agree. So the first priest said: 'For me, it's drink. One night every year, I take off my dog collar, go into mufti, and I go down to the local pub and get totally smashed. Then, the next day, I put the collar back on and I'm fine for the rest of the year. What about you?' The second priest said: 'Well, I must admit that I do like to gamble. One night every year, I take off the collar, take a little cash from the poor box, collect all of the candle money, and I hit the local casino. I blow it all in one evening of gambling. Then, the next day, I put the collar back on and I'm fine for the rest of the year. Now, what about you?' The third priest said: 'For me, it's women and sex. One night every year, I take off my collar, go down to Soho and go after it all night. Then, the next day, I put the collar back on and I'm fine for the rest of the year. What about you?' The fourth priest squirmed uneasily in his chair: 'Well, I guess my biggest sin is that I am a compulsive gossip, and I can't wait to get off this train!'

*

A priest and a rabbi take the same compartment on a train. They look warily at each other and then start reading their respective papers. After a short time, the priest looks up, coughs and says: 'Excuse me, Rabbi, but just as a matter of interest, have you ever eaten pork?' The rabbi, looking a bit guilty, replies: 'Why do you ask?' The priest says: 'Oh, come on, just between you and me, call it professional interest – it won't go any further.' The rabbi says: 'Well, all right then, yes, I did – once – eat pork.' The priest smiles: 'Nice, isn't it!' And he sits back with a smug expression on his face. A few minutes later, the rabbi looks up and says: 'Excuse me, Father, but just between you and me, have you ever had sex with a woman?' Now the priest looks a bit furtive. The rabbi adds: 'Purely for professional interest, you understand – it'll go no further.' So the priest says: 'Well, yes, I did have sex with a woman – only ONCE though!' The rabbi smiles: 'Nicer than pork, don't you think?'

*

A drunk comes out of a bar, and is accosted by a nun standing by the door. She admonishes him and tells him how bad drink is for his brain and his body and his soul. He stops her and says, 'What are you talking about? Have you ever had a drink in your life?' She says, 'No, I have not.' So the drunk says, 'Then how can you criticise me if you haven't experienced it?' So the nun thinks for a minute and then agrees to try a drink, but she asks, 'What drink do ladies drink?' The drunk says, 'Gin.' The nun says, 'All right, I'll do it, I'll try some gin, but have them put it in a cup so no one will notice.' So the drunk goes back into the bar, orders a Guinness for himself and 'a gin in a coffee cup'. The bartender yells, 'It's that bloody nun again, isn't it!'

*

My church accepts all denominations – fivers, tenners, twenties . . .

*

A Catholic teenager goes to confession, and, after confessing to an affair with a local girl, is told by the priest that he can't be forgiven unless he reveals who the girl is. 'I'm very sorry, Father, but I promised not to tell.' The priest asks: 'Come on, my son, tell me: was it Mary Patricia, the butcher's daughter?' The teenager replies: 'No, Father, and I said I wouldn't tell.' The priest then asks: 'Was it Mary Elizabeth, the printer's daughter?' The teenager says: 'No, Father – and I still won't tell!' The priest tries one more time: 'Was it Mary Francis, the baker's daughter?' The teenager is having none of it: 'No, Father!' The priest sighs: 'Well, my son, I have no choice but to excommunicate you for six months.' Outside, the boy's friends ask him what happened. 'Well,' he says, 'I got six months, but three good leads!'

*

Farmer McCarthy lived for many years with only his dog for a companion. One sad day, he found his dog dead from old age. So he went to his parish priest and asked if services could be said for his dog. The good father said, 'Oh no, I'm sorry, we can't have services for a dog here, but there's a new church down the street that might be willing.' 'Father, do you think £50,000 might be enough of a donation?' the farmer asked. 'Well, man,' exclaimed the priest, 'why didn't you tell me your dog was a Catholic?'

*

The Pope is celibate, right? And he tells billions of people throughout the world about their sex life: 'The sole purpose of the sexual act is not pleasure – it is to propagate: to bring Catholic children into the world. No birth control! No use the pill! No use the rubber! No use the Dutch-a cap!' I say to him: if you don't play the game, don't make the rules!

*

There's a little Jewish fella praying in the synagogue, saying: 'God, God help me, my son went to Israel and became a Christian!' And a voice from Heaven says: 'It's funny you should say that . . .'

~

Political
Politicians have developed their own lunatic language. Politics-speak. For example, they'll often double up on things: like they won't say 'I', they'll say 'I myself'; well, if you say 'I' then that's enough, you don't have to say

'I myself' – I know it's you. 'Speaking for myself': that's another one. Of course you're speaking for yourself – so just speak! I actually heard one of them say the other week: 'Speaking for myself, personally . . .' And even worse was this: 'Before I speak, I'd like to say a few words . . .' Another one: 'I am without doubt absolutely convinced.' Moronic! Absolutely moronic! And some of them keep on repeating things, like: 'I will not cease. I will not stop. I will not halt. And I shall continue'. What in the name of Christ are they talking about? They also use words that nobody else uses any more, like 'whomsoever,' 'wherewithal' and 'notwithstanding'. 'Nay': I actually heard one of them come out with that recently. 'Nay'! Who's writing their speeches – Jane Austen?

*

They all call themselves 'Honourable'. What crap! The only people who aren't allowed to enter into Parliament are certified lunatics and convicted criminals. You'd think it was the other way round. I've listened to them in Parliament. I've seen them. I thought, when I first went to the English Parliament, that I'd hear wonderful oratory, learned debate, great discussions, passionate arguments, flashes of wit and verbal swordplay. You been in there? It's like the Fourth Form in a bad grammar school. Like a load of kids. And in charge of them is someone called 'Mr Speaker'. He looks like a demented transvestite poodle! His total vocabulary appears to consist of: 'Ord-er! OR-DER!

OR-DER!!!' It's like having a seal down the other end of the room!

*

We have the 'brain drain' in this country. All the parties say that they're worried by what they call the brain drain. The best brains in Britain are leaving. Does anybody here know of a politician who has left this country in the last ten years?

*

You can always tell the way a person votes by the paper they read. For example, *The Times* is read by people who run the country. The *Financial Times* is read by people who own the country. The *Daily Mail* is read by the wives of the people who own and run the country. The *Daily Mirror* is read by the people who think they run the country. The *Guardian* is read by the people who think that they should run the country. The *Morning Star* is read by the people who think that the country should be run by another country. The *Daily Express* is read by the people who think that the country should be run as it was. The *Daily Telegraph* is read by the people who think that it still is. And the *Sun* is read by the people who don't care who runs the country as long as they've got big boobs.

*

It might appear that I'm being slightly hard on politicians, but in actual fact I've got a very soft spot for all of them. It's a bog in the west of Ireland.

*

In Ireland we don't have politics. If we did, we'd naturally be against 'em.

~

Military

The scene is a battlefield in some war-torn country. A US Army Sergeant is crouched in a dug-out in front of his men, shortly before they're due to go over the top: 'All right, then: two minutes to zero. You okay, Smith? Kowalski? Morelli? Palmer? You two guys over there okay? All right. Just before we go, a few words. You all know how vitally important this mission is. You also know that our chances of coming out of it alive are zero. But you six men have been chosen because you're six men who love to fight. And I couldn't hope to have, er, five better men than, er, you four. It's not only that you're men who love to fight but also that, if you believe in something as strongly as you, er, three do, and are prepared to give up your lives, it makes me feel proud to stand here beside, er, you two, knowing that the pair of us will do this for God and Country. If this mission is successful . . . Hey – wait for me!'

~

Detours and Diversions

These two priests, they're getting a tiny bit jaded and frustrated, so they decide to go to St Tropez on vacation and live a little. They're determined to make this a real vacation by not wearing anything that would identify them as clergy. So as soon as the plane lands, they head straight for a store and buy some really bright, colourful, outrageous-looking shorts, shirts, sandals, sunglasses – the whole range. The next morning, they go to the beach, dressed in their 'tourist' outfits. And they are sitting on their beach chairs, enjoying a drink, soaking up the sunshine and the scenery, when, suddenly, a drop-dead gorgeous young blonde – topless – in a thong bikini comes walking straight towards them. They can't help but stare. And, as she passes them, she smiles and says: 'Good morning, Father! Good morning, Father!' Nodding and addressing each of them individually. Then she passes on by. The two priests are stunned. How in the world did she know that they were priests? The next day, they go back to the store and they buy even more garish and outrageous outfits. These ones are so loud that you can hear them before you've even seen them. Once again, the two priests settle on the beach in their chairs to relax, have a drink and enjoy the sunshine. After a while, the same gorgeous topless blonde comes walking toward them. Again, she nods at each of them, says, 'Good morning, Father! Good morning, Father!' and then starts to walk away. One of the priests can't stand it any longer and calls out: 'Just a minute, young lady!' She stops and smiles and says: 'Yes?' He says: 'Both of us are priests, and we're proud of it, but I *have* to know: how in the *world* did you know that we are priests when we're dressed as we are?' She says: 'Because, Father, it's me – Sister Angela.'

Attempted Reinventions

The most dogmatic person in the world is the person who has been converted from one religion to another. They spend their life trying to impress upon other people the strength of their belief and, if possible, to convert people to their new-found faith. There was a Jewish fella, actually, who became a convert to Catholicism. (I suppose that was how it all started.) So this Jewish fella becomes a Catholic, and after about three years of doing very good work he has an audience with the Pope. Not only does he have an audience with the Pope, but he has a *private* audience with the Pope. And he's in there not only for five minutes, for ten minutes, for half an hour, for an hour, two hours, three hours – this has never happened before, and all the cardinals are racing up and down the corridor, worried! And eventually one looks through the keyhole, and the Pope is sitting on his throne saying: 'Mr Fingelstein, I *am* a Catholic!'

~

Old Habits . . .

There's a story about a man who for years toured the old Variety halls doing his song and dance act. And eventually, as the bookings dried up, he committed a crime and was sentenced to ten years in jail. And it nearly drove him mad. He schemed, and he thought, and, in time, he made an attempt to escape. After two years, he finally got through the bars, dropped down into the big yard below and ran across the ground. And all of a sudden: *Beeeeeee-Baaaaaaw!* The escape's been spotted. A big searchlight picks him out by the fence. He's frozen to the spot for a few seconds, and then he opens his eyes wide, clears his throat, puts his hands out and goes: 'Dum-Dum-Ba-Dumdy-Dum . . . You are my one, true, lady love . . .'

~

Breaking Out of the Prison House of Language

There's a whole snobbery in our language about the professions that becomes more evident the more that you progress. For example, on television, newscasters read 'autocue'; politicians 'refer to their notes'; television hosts of things like game shows will read 'cue cards'; and actors will have 'prompt pages'. But comedians? '*Idiot boards*'! But we shouldn't allow ourselves to become snobbish or stuck in our ways about language. Adults tend to take it too seriously. We should play games with language. We should try to break the rules occasionally, or allow it to happen in the language itself. I was in Lancaster recently, and I went past this hairdresser's, and the name of the hairdresser's was 'Curl Up and Dye'. Now, that's nice. It makes you smile. I've also seen a poodle parlour called 'Pride and Groom', another one called 'Paws for Thought' and I may have seen a taxidermist's called 'Get Stuffed & Up Yours'. There was a shoe shop in Oxford

Street in London called 'R. Soles'; I bought a pair of his shoes – so R. Soles to him, too! But if you actually take that train of thought onwards: an undertakers would be 'His & Hearse'; you could call a bank 'A Place of Interest' or 'Buy Myself a Loan'; the House of Commons would be 'The House of MP Promises'; the House of Lords would be 'God's Waiting Room'; the Ministry of Fisheries would be 'Finders Kippers'; the Welsh Office would be 'Whitehall Leeks'; and the Scottish Office would be the 'Ministry of Sporran Affairs'; and Family Planning would be 'Buy Me and Stop One'.

You know that certain words, within certain professions, are used to imply that somebody's got the sack? For example: a nurse will be 'deregistered'; barristers will be 'debarred'; priests will be 'defrocked'. So what about other professions? Would clerks be 'defiled'? Would musicians be 'decomposed'? MPs 'dismembered'? Economists 'deflated'? Heavy drinkers 'delivered'? Magicians 'disillusioned'? Secret agents 'despised'? Cowboys 'deranged'? Electricians 'delighted'? I suppose prostitutes would be 'delayed'. You can play around with collective nouns, too: you know, like there's always a 'bunch' of grapes or a 'pride' of lions or a 'gaggle' of geese or whatever? So would you get a 'cast of plasterers'? Or a 'horde of misers'? A 'body of morticians'? A 'lot of sodomites'? A 'brace of dentists'? A 'rash of dermatologists'? A 'clutch of drivers'? A 'mass of priests'? How about a 'flock of Indian restaurants'? Keep them coming.

~

Live Deep and Prosper

Freedom can be quite tricky if you come to it late. You'd be like the old fella who fell into a vat of Guinness: he knew exactly what to do, but he couldn't make up his mind where to start.

~

6

Growing Old

Go on failing. Go on. Only next time, try to fail better.

Samuel Beckett

~

Late on in his performing career, Dave Allen agreed to try to sum up his life at that stage, in a playful way, for a national newspaper:

Q: What is your idea of perfect happiness?

A: *Being with good friends drinking a glass of champagne to celebrate Ireland winning the World Rugby Cup.*

Q: What is your greatest fear?

A: *Not being with good friends drinking a glass of champagne to celebrate Ireland winning the World Cup.*

Q: With which historical figure do you most identify?

A: *Abraham Lincoln, because we both died in the theatre (but he only did it once).*

Q: What is the trait you most deplore in yourself?

A: *Farting in the bath.*

Q: What vehicles do you own?

A: *An unkempt Volvo.*

Q: What is your greatest extravagance?

A: *Fresh figs and good wine.*

Q: What makes you depressed?

A: *Political sleaze, dishonesty and British Rail.*

Q: What do you most dislike about your appearance?

A: *My ear lobes and hair growing from my ears.*

Q: What is your favourite word?

A: *Poppy.*

Q: Which living person do you most despise?

A: *Mrs Thatcher.*

Q: Which do you consider the most overrated virtue?

A: *Godliness.*

Q: Which words or phrases do you most overuse?

A: *Bollocks, bullshit, fucking idiot and I love you.*

Q: What is your greatest regret?

A: *Not knowing my father as an adult.*

Q: How do you relax?

A: *Painting, a steam bath or cooking for friends.*

Q: What single thing would improve the quality of your life?

A: *No junk mail.*

Q: What would your motto be?

A: *Never do today what you can put off till tomorrow.*

Q: What keeps you awake at night?

A: *Prince Charles's helicopter and a barking dog.*

Q: How would you like to die?

A: *In extreme old age.*

Q: How would you like to be remembered?

A: *For being older than Methuselah.*

The last couple of answers now hurt, because we lost him far too soon, but, during the period when he responded to this questionnaire, Dave Allen really was growing old quite brilliantly as a comedian.

No other comic engaged with the ageing process as keenly and completely as Dave Allen did once the first fleck of grey caught his eye. The observations began in the late 1970s, but they grew bolder and more detailed as each new

Relaxing with the writer Alan Bennett during the making of
the TV play *One Fine Day* (1979).

The Royal Gala Television Performance, BBC TV Centre, 1970
(*left to right*: the cast of *Dad's Army*, Queen Elizabeth II,
Dudley Moore, Huw Wheldon, Dave Allen, Eddie Braben, Ernie
Wise, Eric Morecambe and Vera Lynn).

In his dressing room before one of his hugely successful
stage shows in the 1980s.

'In case you wonder what I do, I tend to stroll around and chat,'
Dave Allen used to tell his audience. 'I'd be grateful if you'd
refrain from doing the same'.

The masterful comic in action, making people think as well as laugh: 'Why - "why" is a wonderful word'.

'I don't ridicule religion. I ridicule some concepts of what people believe religion is. I firmly believe that if anybody wants to do anything in their life, they have the right to do it'.

Launching the suspense collection he edited, *A Little Night Reading*, in 1974: 'It is not so much that I believe in the supernatural,' he said of his interest in such fiction, 'but like many people I have a fear of the tricks my imagination might play on me'.

Samuel L Jackson considered him 'cool,' and Robert
Stephens declared that he could have been a movie star:
Dave Allen was the comic with leading-man looks.

From controversial clocks to turkey pluckers: Dave Allen
photographed by his great friend, Nobby Clark, in London in 1994.

*decade of creeping deterioration commenced. He chroni-
cled every crease, every crack and every crumble, every blur
of the eye and every blank of the mind. Ageing comics such
as George Burns ('At my age flowers scare me') and Bob
Hope ('Where do I want to be buried? Surprise me!') were
cranking out old jokes about growing old, but Dave Allen
was doing something infinitely more interesting than that:
he was reporting on real life.*

*The irony was that growing old made him seem
younger. Ageing, as a subject, inspired him, energised him,
as much as religion had ever done – and it gave him an
even broader audience.*

*He took the subject, explored it and then, as he put it,
'nagged at it for comedy'. He researched each routine (as
he always had done) more assiduously than many post-
graduates research a scholarly monograph: a fresh file
would be started for each new theme, trend or issue, and it
was soon filled close to bursting with newspaper cuttings
collected from a broad selection of countries; annotated
copies of* The Economist, Time, Newsweek, Scientific
American, Psychology Today, *the* Lancet *and* National
Geographic; *articles, charts and bibliographies culled
from a range of specialist professional journals; various
statistical surveys conducted in various parts of the world;
detailed notes taken from radio and television documentaries; lengthy correspondence with experts working in the
most pertinent academic fields; and also page after page of
notes, ideas, drafts and several painstaking self-critiques.
His comedy was constantly renourished by his extraordinary curiosity and insatiable appetite for new knowledge,*

and there was always something pertinent for him to learn, every single day, about the inexorable process of life.

The material that grew out of growing old proved to be some of the freshest, sharpest and most powerful work that Dave Allen ever did. One of his favourite philosophers, Kahlil Gibran, once wrote that 'exaggeration is truth that has lost its temper', and that observation could have been used to capture the character of Dave Allen's stand-up monologues about life in its later phases. When he returned to television with a new series in 1990, it was just him in a pared-down programme. 'As you can see,' he explained to his audience at the start of the opening edition, 'this show has no music, no titles, no actors, no costumes, no sketches. Let's be honest: it's cheap!' What the series did have, however, was something priceless: a full half-hour each week of peerless stand-up comedy.

Some of the routines – about giving up smoking, for example, and serving time – were more like exhilarating comedy riffs, artfully structured but sounding like they were just rolling straight out from his heart. It did what great comedy always does: it surprised, it intrigued, it inspired and, last but definitely not least, it made you laugh long and hard.

Writing about Allen at the start of what would turn out to be his final series, the TV critic Nancy Banks-Smith said that he was like a '20-year-old malt. Very rare and very expensive, I hope, and you'd recognise it with a bucket over your head. Sip for six weeks. Savour, don't swig.' She was quite right. He was a rare treat.

O Tempora, O Mores

Living

Do you realise how dangerous living is now? Do you know that eating food is as dangerous as writing books? Poor old Salman Rushdie. Jesus – if I was a Muslim I'd have been dead years ago!

Communication

There are certain words in our society that have changed totally. I was in America, where a very good friend of mine – an academic, highly intelligent – was walking across Central Park, and he says, all of a sudden: 'Ah *shit!* I've stood in some dog's *doo-doo!*' Now, 'doo-doo' is shit. 'Shit' is not doo-doo. So you have this word, which has lost its total meaning.

Say I drive down from Birmingham to London, and I say to somebody: 'I drove from Birmingham to London.' In England, they'll say: 'Did you really?' In America, I'll say: 'I drove from Maryland to Washington.' They'll say: 'No shit?' My reaction was: 'Yes, I did!'

The Americans use 'shit' for everything now except shit. Marijuana, grass, ganja, call it what you like, it's now called 'shit' in America. I was sitting in a bar in New York, and a fella came over and, out of the corner of his mouth, he said: 'Hey, man – you wanna buy some shit?' What? 'You wanna buy some shit?' *Shit?* 'Yeah. Columbian. Columbia shit!' *Columbian* shit? 'Yeah. It's the best shit in the world!' You bring it all the way up from Columbia?

'Yeah!' Do you have it on you? 'Yeah'. How much do you have on you? 'About three pounds.' You're walking around with three pounds of shit in your pocket? And people give you money for it? How much do you get? 'About fifty dollars an ounce.' Shit! I'd be a millionaire in a week!

*

Some words now are just perverse. Take, for example, some of the words that are used regarding transporting objects from place to place. If it's freight sent by ship then it's a cargo, and if it's freight sent by car then it's a shipment!

*

Words are important, and so is the psychology of wording. Take, for example, the way that words are used now with aeroplanes. Planes are never late. Have you noticed that? They're always 'delayed'. The blame is always shifted. Then there are the hazards. It's only after you've bought your ticket, and you're in the aeroplane and on the runway, that the hostess tells you about all of the things that can go wrong with the aircraft. You sit there strapped in, listening to this, thinking: 'Why the hell didn't you tell me this before?!?'

*

Have you heard about this 'subliminal advertising' they do now? I'd like to complain about the people who do it, but I gather that they're exceptionally hard to see.

*

Alexander Graham Bell invented the telephone. Which was fine. Until he invented the second one.

When I was a child, in the 'olden' days, at home in Ireland, our phone was something that you *looked* at. You never touched it. It was taboo. Off limits. Only to be used for very serious matters or matters of emergency – and then only by adults. This telephone used to sit in our hallway like a black god. And we all used to talk about it in servile, reverential tones. As a three-year-old I used to tip-toe past the bloody telephone! If it rang I'd *wet* myself!

The attitude to telephones has changed enormously over the years. Now we all have telephones. We're all aware of telephones, we react to telephones, we're blasé about telephones.

We've developed answering machines. Machines to answer machines! The first thing you do when you come home, you listen to your answering machine. And there'll be a message: 'So-and-so rang, will you please ring such-and-such a number.' And you do. And you talk to *his* machine!

Have you ever noticed that wrong numbers are never engaged? You'll always get through to a wrong number.

People actually think that public telephones don't work because they're vandalised. I think they've been vandalised because they don't work.

Do you know the only sure way to prevent a public telephone box from being vandalised? Go in there and vomit and urinate!

Talk about 'advanced' technology: do you know that

they have telephones for the *deaf* now? They don't ring. They just light up. So the deaf person can see that there's somebody on the phone. They pick it up and say: 'Hello . . . Hello . . . Hello?'

Now we have all of these useless services on the telephone. We have things like 'Dial-a-Joke' or 'Dial-a-Poem' or 'Dial-a-Prayer' or 'Dial-a-Blessing'. 'Dial-a-Dirty Phone Call'! You can actually dial dirty phone calls! Years ago they'd *fine* you for doing that. Now they're *paying* you to bloody do it! You can sit there on the telephone and pant, fantasise and masturbate yourself to your heart's content – all for 28 pence a minute! I suppose that when you're finished you can phone 'Dial-a-Confession' – Catholics are into all the money makers!

At one time phones were rare. Now they're everywhere in our society. Mobile phones are now the in-thing. I wander around London, I sit on the tube, I sit on a bus, a train, wherever I am, and I'll see these people, they'll open a briefcase or a handbag or a satchel and out this thing will come: *Babble-babble-babble.* You see them in the streets, walking up and down the streets, talking on their mobile telephones: 'Yeah, yeah, I'd, um, personally I'd keep it to my chest if I were you, I wouldn't let them know *mumble mumble mumble* ha-ha-ha-ha!' And I'm dying, I'm waiting, I'm praying, 'Oh, please, God' – I go to church, I light candles – I'm going, 'Oh, *please*, God, let one of those bastards walk into a lamp-post!'

*

People are more likely to just shout stuff out at you nowadays. Hecklers. My favourite retort to a heckler is: 'If I had a head like yours, I'd have it circumcised!'

*

On television, there's been what I call an 'Americanisation' of audiences. They now do those extraordinary *sounds* all the time. A performer will walk on and he'll say: 'Good evening!' And they all go: *'Woo! Wow! Hoo-Hoo! Yow!'* Jesus, what's all that about? Then the performer will say something like: 'It's wonderful to be here!' And they'll go: *'Wow-Wee! Whoop! Woo-Woo! Yow-Wee!'* All the performer does is say hello and piss off and he's done half an hour!

Service
Receptionists in dentists and doctors now: they *protect* the dentist or doctor. I'd like to see the doctor, please. *'Why?'* Well, I was hoping he'd help me change the tyres of the bloody car!

Crowds
Strange thing about the world today: no matter where you go in the world there are crowds. Totally crowded. I mean, even in graveyards there isn't room to breathe.

Statistics
Governments surround themselves with statisticians these days. I read that one of these statisticians has

worked out that if the Chinese nation, now that they've reached one thousand million, decided to walk around the world in rows twelve deep it would take me fifty-two years of my life to count them as they went by my front door. Now, I don't think that the Chinese are that stupid! I don't think that the whole of the Chinese nation is one day going to stand up and say: 'Oh, I go for walk round world – you come?' They're going to pass by my front door? They all know where I live?

I mean, I've read some extraordinary statistics put out by these people. I read recently that somebody has worked out that 66 tonnes of dog excrement is excreted out on to the streets of Britain! How do they *get* these figures? I mean, can you imagine paying money to educate your child, and he goes on to university and he takes degrees, and he's now the greatest expert in the country on dog crap! He spends all his days wandering around the streets with little rulers and measures!

Gadgets

I was with a friend of mine in his house recently, and he went and stood in the middle of the room and whistled. I said: 'Are you all right?' He went: '*Sssh!*' And then he started whistling again. I said: 'What are you whistling for?' He said: 'My keys.' I said: 'Your *keys?*' He said: 'Yes, when I whistle at them, they let me know where they are.' How do they do that? Do they go: 'I'm hiding in the kitchen – come and find me!'

*

It's lunacy. I was at a funeral recently. And I'm watching the coffin being lowered into the ground. And from inside the coffin, something suddenly goes: *Beep-Beep-Beep-Beep!* I said to the widow: 'What was that?' She said: 'Oh, that was to remind him to take his pills.'

*

You get alarm clocks now that are terribly polite. They repeat everything. They're like Mormons. When one wakes you up in the morning you shout at it. It goes: 'Good morning! This is your alarm call! This is your alarm call! This is your alarm call!' You go: '*Shaddup! Shaddup!*' And it stops! The next time you ask it what time it is it probably goes: 'Promise not to shout at me?'

Queues
I'll tell you who I hate. Queue jumpers. The English are so polite, you tolerate it. I've stood in queues and a fella's nipped in. I go: 'Eh? Eh! *Oi!* Hey, you! *You!*' The fella goes: 'What?' I'll say: 'There's a queue. We're all *queuing!*' And he goes: 'Oh? Oh! I'm sorry. I didn't notice it.' And I'll go: 'You didn't notice it? Eight people standing behind each other? What did you think it was – a gang bang?'

Hairdressers
There's always that moment of truth when you go to the hairdressers. That moment when they've finished with you, and they take the mirror down and they hold it around the back of your head. We all think the same thing. We're all thinking: '*WHAT THE FUCK HAVE*

YOU DONE TO MY HEAD? But then, when they say, 'How's that?' you say, 'Er, yes, thank you.' And then you pay these arseholes and give them a tip! And six weeks later you go back there because you know them!

Shit

When I was a kid in Ireland, I always walked in cow shit. Now I'm a man in London, it's dog shit. It's extraordinary. If there's a piece of dog shit on the streets of London, my feet home-in on it like a bloody Polaris missile! I live in a street in London: it's bloody Turd Terrace! Why don't dogs just come in my house and shit inside and cut out the middle man? I live near Holland Park. There's a sandpit about eight feet by ten feet with a sign saying: 'DOG LAVATORY'. I do not know of any dog in the world that can read English!

Recycling

Everything's being recycled these days: bottles, metal, paper . . . I wonder whether they'll ever recycle condoms? They do it with rubber tyres. 'Retread condoms – guaranteed for twenty thousand miles!' I read recently that, because of the population explosion, certain organisations are now distributing green condoms. Green condoms! I'll give you a word of advice: never wear one of those in the kitchen when your wife's doing the vegetables.

The Festive Season

Christmas is becoming much more stressful. Years ago, I could actually deal with things like, say, Christmas tree lights. I'm one of those people who don't bring their tree into the house until Christmas Eve. The lights work perfectly. Looks beautiful. Two hours before the shops close: every little bastard light goes *bang!* And for the next two hours, I am scampering like a demented lunatic around London searching madly for one little green Christmas tree light that was made in Taiwan in 1967!

It's not only difficult to get a Christmas tree. It's even more difficult to get rid of the bloody thing! Have you tried to get rid of one at the end of Christmas? The dustman won't take it. You can't burn it because you live in a smokeless zone. So you find yourself, after Christmas, creeping surreptitiously around your neighbourhood trying to find a builder's skip. But you can't find one. So you dump it in somebody's garden. You think: 'Thank Christ! Got rid of it!' Then you come back to your own house and there are two Christmas trees dumped in *your* garden!

Why can't the manufacturers of wrapping paper make wrapping paper so large that it can wrap up *two* presents? Why is it always just one-and-a-half? It's actually got to the point now that I buy presents to fit the paper.

The other thing that I notice about Christmas these days is that you buy a box of crackers, and it says: 'Made in Great Britain, with foreign parts.' Aren't we all?

The thing about crackers: it's the hats you get in them. Why can't they fit? You either get them slipping over your eyes, or they sit right up there perched on the top of your head! Who do they test these hats out on? Are there two fellas in Singapore, sitting in some little sweat shop, one with an enormous head and one with a head measuring 3⅞?

Then there's the indoor fireworks. *Indoor fireworks!* 'The Serpent'. You light it: *phiiiiffft – BINGO!* – a dog turd. It looks exactly like a dog turd! 'Mount Vesuvius' – another dog turd! 'Hot-Air Zeppelin' – a flying dog turd!

This really is the silly season for gifts. Somebody actually gave me a pen that writes underwater! I mean, in the first place, why would I *want* to write underwater? If I was underwater, what would I be writing – 'I'm drowning'? On the other hand, if I was underwater writing, what would I write *on* – soggy paper?

The dolls they make now: they really are extraordinary. They walk, they talk, they can urinate . . . I was looking at one the other day that actually *chews*. It comes together with this kind of mushed-up type of food, and the child can actually feed it, and the jaws work, and it has a digestive system, and eventually it all comes out in the nappy. And the child takes it off the nappy and then it goes through the whole process again. It's rather like eating a Big Mac!

~

Retirement

I retired. I still am retired. But to keep myself during my retirement in a manner to which I'm accustomed, I have to work. It's a kind of Irish retirement.

~

Adaptive Self-Delusion

You tend to protect yourself from the ageing process by seeing yourself at a different age. And this happens to us all. We all see ourselves at the age where we feel most suited. I walk down the road, and I'm fifty-three, and I think to myself: 'Maybe thirty.' That's how I think: 'Thirty.' And I'm going down the road swinging. Thirty years old. That's how I see myself. And then I see myself reflected in the shop window. There's a moment of recognition. And then I think: 'Who's that old bastard over there?'

~

Regrets

I don't envy the young their youth or their future. What I envy is their *energy*. I mean, we in the older generation, we try to conserve our energy; they waste it! I walk up the stairs, younger people race pass me: *bam-bam-bam-bam!* I carefully descend stairs, they go past: *wham-bang-crash-wallop!* It's like a bloody mountain goat's just gone by me! It's rather like being somebody with limited spending watching somebody who's got an open cheque book. I don't mind them having the energy, but they don't know how to *use* it. *I* know how to use it, but I don't have it!

*

I think that the ageing process would be much more interesting if, instead of being born young and growing old, you were born old and became young. Then you'd know how to deal with your youth when you got there. You'd have all the energy to do the right things. You wouldn't *lose* hair – on the way back you'd *grow* hair! Your teeth would come back. Your eyesight would come back. All those wrinkles would disappear. And you'd finish up getting breastfed. Jesus – what a way to go out!

*

There were these three old men on a train. They were constant travelling companions, but, on this particular journey, they all expressed their regrets at getting old. 'You know,' the first man started, 'I really regret losing my hearing. I used to really love listening to Beethoven, Brahms and Bach, but as I've got older my hearing has grown worse and worse.' The second old man says: 'I know how you mean. My eyes are starting to go. I used to love going to the art museum and seeing all the Renoirs and Monets, but now I can barely see anything at all.' The last old man nods his head in sympathy: 'Yes, me too. As you both know, I recently married a sweet young thing thirty years my junior, and, every morning, I roll over and ask, "Shall we make love?" and she says, "We just did!" My memory . . .'

Growing Old

Consolations

Some people do object to getting old. I don't. Not when you consider the alternative.

*

One of the good, honest things about growing old is that I don't actually have to 'prove' my masculinity – whatever that means – any more. I'm actually quite happy to say that it now takes me all night to do once what I once did all night.

~

New Resolutions

Stop Smoking

I have given it up. I, a heavy smoker – I used to even smoke *in between* smokes – have given it up. Totally changed. And the most extraordinary thing about giving up smoking is: to non-smokers, I'm a convert, I've come over, I've joined them – they're proud of me. They say: 'Good for you! You've given up the filthy habit! Good-good-good-good!' To the heavy smokers, who used to be my allies, I'm a traitor – 'Bloody Judas! You of all people!'

But one of the good things – or one of the new things – about giving up smoking is that I now have my sense of smell back. I can actually get up in the morning and open the window, throw it open, and breathe in, and smell again! Petrol. Carbon monoxide. Dog shit. Then there's taste: I actually thought when I used to eat food it was because of smoking that I had no taste. It's not the smoking – it's the food! It's bloody tasteless! Somebody said to me the other day, 'Shall we eat or have a McDonald's?'

Actually, being a smoker is very difficult in today's society, because the pressures are on smokers. Society *frowns* upon smokers – there are *signs* everywhere: 'NO SMOKING!' 'SMOKING IS NOT ALLOWED!' 'SMOK- ING IS FORBIDDEN!' The Americans, they're totally lunatic about it. When I was in America I was smoking, and a woman stopped me in the street and she said, 'You're *smoking!*' Like I'd *exposed* myself! I said, 'Yes, madam.' She said, 'You have a *cigarette* in your mouth!' I said, 'Yes, I know, I've been smoking for years – that's the only way I know how!' Have you ever noticed, in public, if you actually spit in the street you can be fined £25? If your dog fouls the footpath: £20. But the cost of a smoke, or what it would cost you if you were *caught* smoking, can be £50. Now that means you can actually have a good spit, your dog can crap to his heart's con- tent, and you've still got a fiver to take home!

When I started smoking, I was actually four-and-a- half. I did it to keep up with my brothers, who were slightly older – I had one brother of six and one who was eight, and they were heavy smokers. So I used to keep up with them and smoke. I'm four-and-a-half, I'm this size *[Lowers a hand down to about three feet from the ground]*, and people would say: 'It'll stunt your growth!'

Everybody in school smoked. As soon as there was a

school break we'd all go to the lavatory. In the cubicle. Eight or nine of us in each cubicle, passing this little cigarette along *[Puff! Puff! Puff!]*. If you went out and looked down the line of cubicles it was like the Industrial Revolution! If somebody used them for what they were intended to be used for it was like a breath of fresh air!

But, you see, nowadays the attitude has changed. Nowadays, smoking is considered to be a dirty habit practised by the minority. When I started to smoke, however, it was regarded as a relaxing pastime and was practised by practically everybody. Everybody smoked. Anybody who was anybody smoked. Politicians smoked. Sportsmen smoked. Film stars.

Did you ever go to the cinema years ago, when there were no smoking regulations? Everybody in the cinema smoked! It was just a mass of smoke. You'd go in and you'd be going *[Waving both hands in front of his face]*, and when you got to the screen and could see the screen, people on the screen were going *[Mimes puffing on a cigarette]*. Do you remember those scenes, those seduction scenes? How the cigarette was *played* with? How it became part of a kind of *hand phallic symbol*? People would touch it and stroke it. Women would put it into their mouth and take it out again – the whole audience would go *[Look of astonishment]*. They used to have those cigarette cases that you could buy that, when you pressed the button, one cigarette came out all by itself. It was a sexual invitation! You'd hand it to her and the cigarette would go *[Mimes a cigarette erection]*, and if the woman went *[Mimes the cigarette being shoved back down from whence it came]* you'd go *[Grimaces]*.

Do you smoke after you've made love? I don't mean literally. Most smokers, straight after they've made love, go: 'I love you, darling.' 'Oh yes, that was beautiful.' 'Oh, yes, oh yes, you were marvellous, it was wondrous' – and yet you can't get to the cigarettes quickly enough! *[Puff! Puff!]* 'Can we do it again?' 'Er, yes, gimme a minute *[Puff-Puff]*.' Do you remember Clark Gable? Clark Gable used to do that thing where he'd light *two* cigarettes at the same time. He'd put two of them in his mouth, light them both, then he'd lean across to the female and she'd take one of them and put it in *her* mouth – and within two minutes they're in bed! I'm sixteen years of age, I'm at a dance hall in Dublin, so I'm going up to females saying, 'Like a cigarette?'

But a couple of years ago I decided I would give up smoking. Because I have teenage children, and I knew that, one day, my teenage children were going to come in smoking, and I didn't actually think that I could be hypocritical enough to sit there and watch them go *[Puff!]* and I'm going *[Puff!]* 'Don't do that! It's a *filthy* habit – give it to me!'

So I thought: 'How? How difficult is it to give up?' And I heard about these substitute cigarettes. Have you seen them? It's a kind of little plastic tube with a fake filter tip at the end, and when you feel you want one you suck on it. It's like breastfeeding. I got totally addicted to them – I was going through sixty a day!

Acupuncture: I inquired about acupuncture. What

they do with acupuncture is they put little needles in your ears, and when they take the needle out they put a little cat-gut chord in there. And when you feel the urge you just go *[Twiddles an ear lobe]*. What a load of crap!

Hypnosis. What they do with hypnosis is they put you under a kind of light hypnotic trance, and they'll get an ash tray and fill it up with cigarette ends, and while you're under the trance they'll wave it under your nose and say: 'Now think of it. Think of smoke. Think of the *tar*, the *congestion*, think of the *ash*, breathe in that *smell*, breathe it *all* deep in your *lungs*, think of it . . .' And then they go *click!* 'Come out. Now, what do you think of that?' *[An ash tray full of cigarette stubs is shoved under his nose.]* And you go: 'Er, I'll have that one there . . .'

But I *had* decided that I would give up smoking. What actually happens, when it comes to giving up smoking, is that you're two people: there's the person who *wants* to smoke, and there's a person who *doesn't* want to smoke, so you have a kind of Jekyll and Hyde going with you all the time.

And I woke up one morning, at eight o'clock in the morning, and I sat there and I thought, 'That's it: *this* is actually the day I will give up smoking.' And then I thought, 'But I don't *really* want to give it up. What you should actually do is cut it down. What you should do is think: "You'll only smoke because you enjoy a smoke." Because you like smoking, you get a certain pleasure out of it, but instead of it being unhealthy what you should do is just take the moments when you really get the most enjoyment, and that is the time you smoke. When you enjoy smoking most: after a meal – that is when I enjoy smoking most. Fine. You can have twelve a day.' And I'm actually sitting there at eight o'clock in the morning going *[Puff!]* 'Fine. Twelve. That's good. Right. Let's see, that's twelve cigarettes . . . It's eight o'clock now . . . I won't go to bed before twelve o'clock at night . . . That's sixteen hours . . . Twelve cigarettes . . . That's an hour and twenty minutes between every cigarette . . . *[Puff! Stubs out fag end]* I've finished that one . . . It's only three minutes past eight . . . You've only got eleven cigarettes . . .' The wife comes in:

'Good morning darling!'
'*SHUT UP!*'
'Who's going to drive the children in?'
'*LET THEM WALK!*'

Twelve o'clock noon, I have gone through *nine* cigarettes! I'm a lunatic! I'm sitting there going: 'Oh my *God!* *[Sobs]* Twelve hours! God, *please* help me! No, wait, wait: you have *some* cigarettes . . . You've got three cigarettes left over . . . That's four hours' smoking . . . You can cut 'em in half . . . But that'll be two dog-ends, they'll be two butts, I'll be throwing away more cigarettes . . . No, wait, wait, wait . . .' And I'm trying to explain it to myself. Now here I am: I've been a smoker since I was so big, I am now going through the first withdrawal symptoms I have ever gone through in my life. So I explained this. I said: 'Listen, listen! Wait! Calm down! You are actually experiencing *withdrawal symptoms!* This is your first time. It's *difficult!* We know it – but you've got to *persevere!*

Tomorrow is not going to be so difficult. Because you'll have experienced what it is today so tomorrow it won't be so bad. But you'll still have twelve cigarettes tomorrow and you won't *need* those twelve cigarettes tomorrow! You'll probably only need five or six! Or four! So take those eight today and forget about them!

Stop Secondary Smoking

I'm a convert now. I hate smokers. I *loathe* smokers. If a smoker is sitting beside me I'll say: '*Stick it up yer arse!*' Actually, somebody said to me: 'But *you* were a smoker!' I said: 'Yeah, but I'm *not* a smoker any more!' They said: 'But it's only smoke.' I said: 'But it's *secondary* smoke. I don't want that secondary smoke *in* me.' And they said: 'Well, you *drink*, don't you?' I said: 'Yes, I drink – but I don't *piss* on you, do I?'

Stop Drinking

It's very illogical, actually, when you pick up something that is purely alcohol and say to somebody: 'Good health!' When you actually think about the properties of alcohol. The damage it does to you – it destroys your brain cells, gives you enormous headaches, double vision, DTs, destroys your stomach lining, your bladder, your kidney, your liver. And yet we say: 'Good health!' We say: 'Cheers! Good health! Long life! Happiness!' We should actually be saying: 'Misery! Short life! Bad health!' That whole thing's very odd: I mean, have you ever seen anybody toast somebody with a glass of milk? No! We never pick up anything that's healthy, like a glass of water or a cup of tea, and say: 'Good health!' If you're in a bar, you'll look across, raise your glass and go: 'Cheers! Good health!' But if you were in a café with a cup of coffee, you wouldn't raise it and go: 'Good health!'

*

Drink doesn't affect me tremendously. I mean, if I get stoned out of my head, I'll get into bed, and I'll go fast asleep. But if a burglar were to walk in to my house, I would immediately be alert. I would wake up. My mind would be sharp, concise, clear. I would think: 'Where is my torch? Where is my club?' And then I would think: 'How do I get out of bed?'

~

Intimations of Decrepitude

Hair
People think that grey hair is a sign of ageing. It *can* be a feature of the ageing process, but it's not necessarily *caused* by it. You can become grey because of various different reasons. It can be hereditary. A malfunction of the genes can cause greyness. Anaemia causes greyness. Lacking vitamin B and vitamin F causes greyness. Vast quantities of liquids can cause greyness *[He glances down sheepishly at the familiar glass that sits by his side]*. Shock causes greyness. Terror, fear, shock can actually cause greyness. It's been recorded that a man went from being totally black-haired to totally white-haired in

something like seven minutes. That's an interesting thing. I mean, I'm going grey on the top of my head, but the rest of my body hair is black. My eyebrows are black, my beard is black, the hair on my hands, legs and chest is black. I did notice recently, when I was having a bath, that I had my first white pubic hair. Now, what did *he* see that the others *didn't* see? Can you imagine one of those little dark hairs turning round to the grey hair and asking him, 'Wh-what did you see?' 'I-I saw –' '*EEEEK!*' Another one. Now there are *two* greys!

*

I don't know if it's a change in metabolism, but the texture, the quality, of the hair, over the years, changes itself. It becomes more coarse and hard. For example, years ago, all my eyebrows were uniform in length. Then about three or four years ago, I was just sitting there talking to someone as you casually do, and I'm just stroking my eyebrows. And I suddenly come across a hair that doesn't *belong* in there. I just pulled it and – *Christ!* – it was about an inch-and-a-half long! A bloody hair! Now, that was abnormal, at that time. Now it's the norm! All the little ones have gone. My eyebrows are shooting off in all directions: half an inch, a quarter of an inch, an inch . . . Isn't it amazing?

My ears – which years ago had no hairs in them – now have *forests, clumps and bushes* not growing into my ears but coming *out* of my ears! My nose is a hirsute factory! They just keep on descending like a bloody forest! I have to attack them with scissors and tweezers.

What in the name of Christ is happening to my body? I'm losing hair off the top of my head and it's coming out of every orifice in my body!

*

I was reading about baldness. Do you know, they tell you that if you go bald from the front of the head, you're a great thinker? And they say that if you go bald from the back of your head, it's because you're sexy? I guess that means that if you go bald at the front and the back of your head at the same time, you're just thinking about it.

Eyesight

Your eyes start to change. They suddenly go. It's an extraordinary thing. You don't realise it's your eyesight – I actually thought that it was something to do with my arms! I mean, I'd pick up a book and I go *[Squints as he holds the book further and further away from his face]*. So I went to see an optician, and he explained in that knowledgeable way that they all have – arseholes! – that it's just a 'natural' change: 'It's your body evolving – it's Nature's way of protecting you.' What the hell is *that* all about? Why do you need to see things that are further away when you're old? Surely you need to see the things that are bloody nearer to you! Like the steps. Kerbs. Other pedestrians. Lamp-posts. I can see the bus at 300 yards – I can't find the bus stop.

I went to see this optician. I got my glasses. I got my first pair of glasses. Do you know the most amazing thing about getting your first pair of glasses? As soon as you get these glasses, your bloody memory goes! I put my glasses on, take them off – in just a second I have no idea where they are! I'm walking around like a dickhead going: 'Er . . . Where . . . Wh-Where are my glasses?' I actually spend half of my life, in my diminishing years, looking for bloody glasses! I write myself little notes now: 'Your glasses are on the mantel shelf.' I find the note but I can't read it – I've got no bloody glasses! My children – who are caring, concerned, loving children – have lost all patience with me. While I'm looking for my glasses I'm groping around like an idiot, whimpering like a fool: 'Have you seen my glasses . . . ?' 'Oh, for *Christ's* sake, Daddy! You geriatric old *fart!* They're *there* – right in *front* of you, right under your *nose!* Can't you *see* them?' 'If I could bloody see them I wouldn't need them!'

What I do now is, when I take them off, I put them far away so I can see them.

*

The eyesight's going. They say it's the first thing to go. I *hope* it is.

*

The optician, he said to me: 'How about contact lenses?' I can't even find the big bastards – how would I find those little ones?

~

Age and Attitude

Age not only changes you physically. It changes your attitude, too. For example, around 1950, there was a movie made called *Sunset Boulevard* by Billy Wilder. And it starred a lady called Gloria Swanson. And in it she played a sixty-year-old lady who had been a star of the silent screen. And she picks up a destitute young writer and turns him into her playboy. And there's a scene in this movie where she seduces him into her bed. And she's sixty-odd years of age. Now, I'm in the cinema, I'm seventeen years of age at the time, and she's lying there, with her face a mass of make-up. She's got eyelashes that look like caterpillars running across her face. She holds up her arms and they wobble – all that loose flesh going *wobble wobble!* Her mouth is like a bloody great slash. And she lies there and she goes: '*KISS ME!*' I'm in the cinema going: '*Yeeeeeoooo-yuk!*' And when he kisses her I go: '*Aggggh!*' *[Vomits]*. Changing attitude: that movie was on television recently. I'm sitting there. They go through that whole scene. She says: '*KISS ME!*' And I'm thinking: 'Shit – I *fancy* her!'

*

I've been going to the pictures all my life, and yet I've still not seen anybody, in the movies, go to the lavatory. I don't mean that I want to see them actually *go* to the lavatory; I just want to *know* that they go. I'd just like to hear somebody say: 'Excuse me, I'm going to the lavatory.' Take a movie like *The Ten Commandments*: there's

Moses and forty thousand Jewish people, and they walk all the way from Egypt to the Promised Land, and yet not one person ever says to Moses: 'Excuse me, Moses – do you mind if I dart behind the hill and have a crap?' *55 Days at Peking*: they do everything – they make love, they kill, they have babies, they dance, they eat – but nobody says: 'I'm just going to the lavatory.' I'm not surprised that the Chinese didn't want the place afterwards! And when you think of a movie like *Gone with the Wind*, you'd think that somebody *would* have done something! Cowboy pictures: how many times have you seen, in cowboy pictures, a sign somewhere in the saloon that says 'LAVATORY' or 'GENTS'? And remember: those cowboys have been eating beans and drinking beer all day, but they don't even fart! (Actually, they do – that's why they're shooting off those guns all the time.) But it's not only the people, it's the animals, too: you see all of those horses, but have you ever looked at the ground? There's nothing on it! I live in the country: I walk five minutes and I find crap everywhere! In movies, you get those great ranches bringing in thousands of cattle: nothing. How do they do it? How do they stop it? Is it like, three minutes before they start shooting the movie, somebody says: 'All right: put the corks in!'

*

As we age, we all have a totally different attitude to the key years in life expectancy. When you're in your teens, ageing's got nothing to do with you; ageing's got to do with other people – *old* people. And then when you're twenty, you kind of think, 'If I live to be forty I'll be happy.' Forty to a twenty-year-old is *ancient*. And then when you're thirty, you're thinking: '*Forty?* Surely I'm entitled to live a few more years than *forty?* How about fifty-five? Go on – give me fifty-five, I'll be happy with fifty-five!' Then, when you get to be fifty-five: 'Seventy-five! *Seventy-five!*' You get to seventy-five and you think: '*Shit! Seventy-six! Please God, SEVENTY-SIX!!!*' Then, when you get to eighty-three, it makes no difference, because you've *gone*: you're into a second childhood, thinking: 'He-he! When I grow up I'm going to be an engine driver! Ha-ha!'

*

There's one of these beautiful English country houses. And there's a huge ball held there, and anybody who's anybody is invited. There's one old lady there, she's ninety-three years old, she's sitting there, and she's had a bit too much of the booze. So she's sitting there, and she thinks to herself: 'I haven't got long to live. And I'm going to do one exciting thing before I die. I'm going to *streak* through the ballroom.' So she goes into a separate room, takes all of her clothes off, opens the door again and goes: *whooosh!* – right through the ballroom! And there's two old fellas sitting there, and one of them asks: 'Who was that?' The other one says: 'I *think* it was Lady Daphne.' The first one says: '*Really?* What was she wearing?' The other one replies: 'I don't know, but whatever it was it needs a bloody good ironing!'

Memory

How pompous in youth we are about memory. I remember years ago, every Christmas, we would have relatives. Ancient relatives. That holy spirit of Christmas and peace on earth and goodwill to everybody. We used to invite all of these idiot aunts that we had. And they all used to sit around, and they'd all talk. And they'd watch television, and there'd be some very interesting movie on, and they'd just talk the whole way through it. They'd talk about it, but they never knew what they were talking about. They'd all go: 'Oooh, er, yes, ah, mmm, yes, she was in that umm, ah, oh yes, she was, yes, and wasn't she married to, er, yes, that was before she went off with the other one, ah, yes!' And I was sitting there thinking, 'You mad old geriatrics – what the hell are you talking about?'

Now, it's me! Now I'm sitting in my own house with my children and I'm going, 'Wasn't he in, er, that, ah . . .'

It's an extraordinary thing, memory. I mean, quite recently – an example of loss of memory – it was in split seconds: I'm in my house. I'm downstairs in my house. There is something that I want which is upstairs. I know what it is, and I know *exactly* where it is upstairs. And I leave the sitting room, I walk across the corridor, go three steps up the stairs, and now I have *no* idea of what it is I'm going up to look for! So I think, 'Well, reason this through. Don't go up and look for something you don't know what you're looking for. Sit down on the stairs, work your way back to the point when you thought what it was you wanted.' In two minutes, I have no bloody idea whether I was upstairs coming down or downstairs going up!

~

But Answer Comes There None

As I get older, I get more curious. I don't mean I get more 'curious', in the sense of strange, I mean I get more curious about things I never used to get curious about. Why? 'Why' is a great question. Why is it, for example, when you hit your knee, or crack your elbow, or stub your toe, you become dumb for about ten seconds? You go: *[Grimaces in silence]*. And yet the only way that you can get rid of that pain is to say: *'SHIT!'* And then it's gone. It's an immediate cure! Have you noticed that?

*

There are other things like, when I'm lying in bed at night asleep – why do I get a cramp? I've not *done* anything. I haven't run a hundred yards or gone up and down the stairs, yet I wake up and I've got bloody cramp! From nowhere! Do you ever make *love* and get cramp in the middle of it? You're making love and suddenly: *'Ha-He-Dee-Ha-Ahh!!'* 'Is it *that* good, darling?' *'NO, I'VE GOT BLOODY CRAMP!'*

*

The 'yips'. I'm interested in the yips. Have you heard about the yips? Sportsmen get the yips. A kind of nervous block of some sort. They can't finish off what they're doing. Dart players get ready to throw their dart and it won't go out of their hand. You see snooker players: they get stuck standing over the ball. Golfers: the same thing. Can you imagine a banker getting the yips? You're in the bank and they won't give you the bloody money! A brain surgeon working on your brain: just hovering over you staring at it! A priest giving you Holy Communion: he keeps on pulling the wafer back! Can you just imagine approaching the climax of love: '*Ah-Ah-Ah-Um . . . Ah-Ah-Ah-Um . . .*'

*

There are all sorts of 'whys'. Why do I hate models in shops? Those mannequins. I hate them! They're always so kind of *languid*. Always so pleased with themselves. That's another thing: I'll see a model, a male model, wearing a suit in a shop window and he looks wonderful – the suit is perfect; I go in, put that suit on – I look like a sack of manure!

*

Here's another 'why'. Why do politicians, whenever they're talking about the educational system, why do they always say: 'The Three Rs'? They always say it: 'The Three Rs: Reading, Writing and Arithmetic.' Bloody bastards can't even spell!

*

There are other things that puzzle me. Why is it that I can never get a whole Brazil nut out of the shell? For bloody years, I've had the crackers, and I've tried and tried, clicked here and clicked there, and I've got it almost perfectly, and then – *crack!* – it's split in half!

*

So many 'whys'. Why do slow drivers always wear hats? Why is it, when people are in their cars, when one person does something, *everybody* has to do it? Sit in your car in a traffic jam and blow your horn. For no reason whatsoever. Just blow your horn. Every driver will assume that you're blowing the horn at him personally. It becomes a total personal affront as far as he's concerned. You just go *Beep!* And watch all the heads in the cars in front of you: they're like demented chickens, darting this way, that way. And then they'll all start: *Beep! Beep-Beep! BEEP!* And why is it that there are certain drivers who can always pre-empt the light going green? Have you ever noticed that? You're there, the light is on red, you're waiting, and just a split second before the light turns from red to green, the fella behind you is on the horn: you're sitting there, it's red – *BEEP!* – it's green – *SHIT!* What I do now, I get irked by it. I stay there. When they go *BEEP!* I'll be looking in the mirror, miming: 'Do you mean *me?* *BEEP! BEEP! BEEP!* And I'll wait until it's gone on red again and then I'll get out of the car and go over to his window: 'Excuse me, but are you trying to *tell* me something?' He'll say: 'The light! Green!' So I'll say: 'Yes, excuse me, but there was an old lady walking in front of my car at the time. Had I known that *you* were in a hurry I would have run the poor old bitch over!'

*

Here's another 'why' about cars. Why is it that when a car is causing an obstruction, they bloody clamp it and *leave* it there?

*

Then there's food. The food in our kitchens. You'll remember this from your childhood. You can remember this from any day of your life. You walk in to the kitchen and you'll say: 'Can I have a glass of milk?' And someone will say: 'Yes, but don't use the fresh one – use up yesterday's.' Or you'll go: 'Can I have a slice of bread?' And they'll say: 'Yes, but use up yesterday's bread.' So you spend all your life eating up bloody stale milk and stale bread!

*

Another thing that confuses me: my breadboard is disappearing. I've had it for about twelve years. It started off about that thick *[signals an inch]*. It's now about this thick *[signals less than half-an-inch]*. Am I *eating* it? The knives – the knives are all thinner, too! What am I doing – eating bloody steel and wood?

*

Then there's the air kiss. Why do women, when they kiss you – I don't mean when they kiss you sexually, I mean when they do so socially for reasons of etiquette – they never actually *kiss* you, do they, they just put their face out and go: '*Myyghur!*' And you get the sound of that '*Myyghur!*' right in your ear! Now, when I meet a woman socially, I tend to kiss her on both sides of the face. Normally. In Britain, sometimes, that doesn't work: I'll kiss her on one side, and then she's off and I'm left kissing thin air! They'll turn around and see me and say: 'What are you doing?' I'll say: 'I was going to kiss you on the other side, too.' They'll say: 'Oh, the French way!' I'll say: 'No! The French way is when you *open* your mouth!'

*

And here's yet another thing: why are we doing away with the most important and enjoyable ingredients in what we eat? I'm Irish, I can't understand the logicality of 'salt-free salt'. What the hell is 'salt-free salt'? Or 'nicotine-free tobacco', or 'caffeine-free coffee'? Christ, coffee is terrible – the only reason that you *have* coffee is to get a *buzz* out of it! If you don't get a buzz out of it, what the hell are you drinking it for? 'Odourless garlic': '*ODOURLESS GARLIC*'! The *joy* of eating garlic is *breathing* on people the next day! 'Alcohol-free booze': for Christ's sake, what is *that*? 'Clear mascara': have you seen that? *CLEAR MASCARA!* I mean, you have mascara to heighten the eyeline: 'Look – I'm wearing an invisible eyeline!' What next? What about sex? What is it going to be: 'Orgasm-Free Sex'?

*

Anti-depressants. When you get depressed, they give you anti-depressants. Do you know what anti-depressants do to you? They make you impotent. You become impotent from anti-depressants. So when you become impotent, you become even more depressed! So they give you more anti-depressants! And you become even more depressed. So you're totally celibate, and depressed and impotent. The only job that's open for you is the Pope!

~

Passing On Your Wisdom

This is a true story about Joyce in Dublin. There was a young American researcher. ABC or CBS were going to do a wonderful, really in-depth, programme for the American market on Joyce. And he was talking to somebody in the hotel, and they said: 'What are you doin' over here?' He said: 'I'm researching Joyce for an American television programme.' The man said: 'Oh, God, that's lovely, that's great, that is. Um, there's a fella, in between Blackrock and Bray, there's a fella there, an old fella, he'll be in one of two pubs. He'll be in Burn's or he'll be in Nolan's. If he's not in one, he's in the other. And he knows more about Joyce than anybody else in the world. So he's worth going out and having a glass of Guinness with.' So the American immediately went out and found this man and sat down and said: 'I believe you know a great deal about Joyce?' The man said: 'Oh, yes. I knew him well, I knew him well. A lovely man.' And he starts to talk about Joyce. And he's giving this researcher – who knows Joyce inside out – he's giving him information he's never heard before! He's telling him things about Joyce that he can barely believe! And at the end of it the researcher says: 'I don't believe it – this is *wonderful* and I've got it all on tape! Can I come back and can I refer to you again?' The old fella says: 'Ah, yes, sure, of course! It's been wonderful to talk. Because nobody likes to talk about the old times. Nobody likes to listen. The young don't want to listen. They don't want to hear. You're a nice young fella, and you've sat down here, and it's been wonderful!' So the researcher says: 'Well, can I pay you?' And the fella goes: 'Oh, no, no, no – the pleasure is in the talking!' So this American says: 'Well, there must be *something* I can do for you? Really, I mean – anything?' And the old fella says: 'Well, there *is* one thing. Er, Joyce . . . He had a son called "James". Could you tell me whatever happened to him?'

~

Tempus Feckit

Time. Time is a transient thing. And yet somehow or other we want to grab hold of it and keep it. We actually, in reality, talk about and say such things as, 'We've got to save time.' You can't *save* time: time's gone. Motor manufacturers will make as a selling point a feature of the car that your car can go from 0 to 60 in 5.8 seconds – thereby saving you 2 seconds. And people actually get wrapped up in this. They talk to each other:

'Does your car *really* go from 0 to 60 in 5.8 seconds?'
'Yes. Yes, it does.'
'I wish I had a car like that! You really save 2 seconds?'
'Yes. Last week I saved a minute and a half!'

It becomes a talking point. You see people racing around the country – they don't *see* the country, they don't *see* things, don't *experience* things, they just get in the car and go off: *Eeeeeeeeeaaaayyyooooow! Eeeeeeeeeaaaayyyooooow! Eeeeeeeeeaaaayyyooooow! Eeeeeeeeeaaaayyyooooow! Beep! Beep! Eeeeeeeee-eaaaayyyooooow!*

People come down from Glasgow:

'I did it in four-and-a-half hours! From Glasgow to London: four-and-a-half hours!'
'Did you really?'
'Yeah!'
'How long does it normally take you?'
'Seven hours! Saved two-and-a-half hours!'
'What did you do with the time you saved?'
'I bored the arse off of people talking about it!'

The kitchen is a great area for time-saving. All of those 'time-saving' devices. Like electric carvers. Why do you need an electric carver? By the time you get the meat out of the oven, and get this thing out of the drawer and plug it in, the bloody meat's freezing! And you can't cut nicely, you can't slice, you can't carve: *Grrrrrrrrrrrr* – 'Wanna leg?' Goes through the bone: *Grrrnnnnnrrraaaagggghh.* Food processors that chop everything up: *chuk-chuk-chuk-chuk-chuk!* Potatoes – *chuk-chuk!* – meat – *sludge-chuk-sludge!* – whip your chocolate up in three seconds – *wheeeeeeeeoooop!* – mayonnaise – *wheeeeeesshh!* It doesn't show you the time it takes to *clean* the bloody thing!

I was in Hong Kong recently, and I was walking by a shop, and I see a watch. And there's nothing there. There's just a black face, there's no hands, no numbers – nothing. And I said, 'What-what is it?' He said, 'Ah, that's a talking clock.' I said, 'A what?' He said, 'A talking clock. It tell you the time.' I said, 'The clock tells you the time?' He said, 'Yes. You walk down road, all you have to do is do that *[flicks wrist]* and pressure of wrist activate speaking for you. Save you all the time of doing that *[lifts up watch to eye level]*. You don't have to do that.' You walk down the road, and a little voice on your wrist says, 'Four Forty-Two! Four Forty-Two and Thirty Seconds!'

Watches are not watches any more. Watches used to be something that you told the time with. Now they're a kind of advanced technological machine. A miracle of engineering. They're not just watches. They're calculators. Computers. People talk about them:

'See this? Extraordinary watch. You see, not only does it tell the time here in London, but you see this little dial over here to the left of the 12? That tells you the time in San Francisco.

This one on the right by the 2 tells me the time in Tokyo and this one down here at the bottom tells me the time in Vancouver. Extraordinary, isn't it? Isn't it wonderful, to be able to tell the time? Do you want to know what the time is in San Francisco?'

'No.'

'You *don't* want to know what the time is in San Francisco?'

'I don't want to know what time it is in San Francisco. I'm in London. What the hell would I want to know what the time is in San Francisco?'

'Oh, how about Tokyo?'

'Piss off!'

It's a calculator. 'Really?' Yes, wonderful! It's a musical box, a memory bank – when's your birthday? 'The sixth of July.' Just a second *[click-click-click]* now wait: *'Happy Birthday to you, Happy Birthday to you, Happy Birthday dear dum-dum, Happy Birthday to you!'*

It's a stopwatch. A *stop*watch! I said, 'What do you need a stopwatch for?' He said, 'Well, it's very handy if I'm doing something and I like to know how long it takes me: when I start it I just press the button, and when I finish I go *[click!]*.' So I said, 'Like what?' He said, 'Well, when I'm making love. When I'm making love, it's very interesting to see how long I take to make love. Just before I enter, I go *[click!]* and when I finish I go *[click!]*: "Hmm: three-and-a-half seconds!"'

It's a compass. 'There's a compass there, you see: North, South, East and West!' *Why* do you want to know? Why do you want to *know?* What do you want a compass for on your watch? He said, 'Well, it's very handy. I like to know where I'm going. Which direction I'm going. When I'm making love, I can go, "North by Northwest. South! South by East. West! *North!*"'

People actually say things like 'It's shockproof'. *Shockproof!* I'm going to get one of those shockproof watches and go 'The Pope's a poof!'

And they'll boast about a watch that can tell you the time at fifty fathoms! Who in the name of Christ is going to ask you what time it is at *fifty fathoms?* You're down there – you're in the murk, the gloom – swimming along. Somebody goes *[muffled voice:]* 'What time is it?' *[Another muffled voice:]* 'It's 10.47! Would you like to know what time it is in San Francisco?'

And I always think about how we *live* by time. How we live by the *watch*, the *clock*. We're brought up to the clock. We're brought up to respect the clock. Admire the clock. Punctuality: we live our life to the clock. Isn't that right? You wake to the clock. You go to work to the clock. You clock-in to the clock. You clock-out to the clock. You come home to the clock. You eat to the clock. You drink to the clock. You go to bed to the clock. You get up to the clock. You go back to work to the clock. You do that for forty years of your life and then you retire. And what do they give you? A fucking clock!

~

Ode to Drink

The horse and the mule live thirty years and
    nothing know of wine and beer
The goats and sheep at twenty die with never
    a taste of scotch or rye
The cow drinks water by the ton and at eighteen
    is mostly done
The dog at sixteen cashes in without the aid of
    rum or gin
The cat in milk and water soaks and then in
    twelve short years it croaks
Yes animals are strictly dry, they sinless live
    and swiftly die
While sinful, ginful, rumsoaked men survive for
    three score years and ten
And some of us, the mighty few, stay pickled till
    we're ninety-two.

~

Hanging On

It really is my ambition just to get old. I just want to get
older and older and older. I want to get my telegram
from the Queen. And then keep going. It's my ambition
to be able to look back on my old age.

*

A little piece of Heaven, was one evening seen a falling,
It hit the Bishop on the head, as he went about a calling,
My God! what is happening he said, before he died.
It's time for you to join me a Heavenly voice, replied.

DA

~

Hedging Your Bets

I'm an atheist. Thank God.

~

Fear of the Unknown

People always want to know what's going to happen to them. They're always looking for the future: they read tea leaves, or they get the cards read to them, or they read the stars, or visit fortune-tellers. There was one man who was terribly worried about whether he would go to Heaven. He went to a fortune-teller and said: 'I want to know if when I die I will go to Heaven.' And she said: 'Cross my palm with silver.' Then she took out the crystal ball. She looked into it, and as she looked into it, it began to cloud over, there was a mist inside the ball, and gradually it began to form into ancient symbols, which she gazed upon, and then they disappeared. And she said: 'You *will* go to Heaven when you die. There's one other thing . . .' He said: 'What?' She said: 'You're going today at 3:45.'

~

7

Death

Evil is even, truth is an odd number,
and death is a full stop.

Flann O'Brien

~

*D*eath: 'the dark backing that a mirror needs if we are to see anything'. Saul Bellow said that, but Dave Allen certainly concurred. Death was always there in his humour, even as far back as during his childhood days, when he started to joke about the nuns and the priests who were trying to fill his head with dark thoughts about what happens before and after the last breath.

He acquired an unusually broad, quasi-anthropological outlook on the various ways in which different cultures, classes and creeds anticipate and respond to the fact of death: some hiding from it, or at least hiding it from them, while others seem keen to embrace it or even fixate on it. He found his comedy not in the absence of the human being, but rather in the presence of the humbug that some sought to put in that person's place. 'I send up situations and institutions that are dear to a good many of my audience,' he admitted. 'But people should realise,' he added, 'that when I poke fun at coffins, I'm not ridiculing death.'

The seed of one of his most famous and best-loved sketches – in which the two separate funeral processions raced each other to the same cemetery – was planted at a very early age, when he was travelling with his mother and brothers on the way back from burying his father in the family grave in suburban Tallaght. The funeral had been a major event by Dublin standards, attracting the likes of Ireland's newly-appointed Taoiseach (the Irish Republic's equivalent of Prime Minister) John Costello as well as the full quota of local journalism's great and good, but, once it was over and the procession of cars set off home, the air of tragedy turned close to farce. Allen recalled: 'Somebody said to the man who was driving the front car, which was an old Rolls that had 120 miles on the speedometer, "God, that car, that car will never do 120 miles an hour!" And the driver said, "No, it won't do 120, but I've gotten 90 out of it before." And the fella says, "A fiver yer won't do 90!" And the [driver of the] second car went, "Where's he goin'?" So he went off at about ninety as well! And suddenly this entourage that had gone off very slowly is now coming down the road at about ninety miles an hour!'

Dave Allen went on to make innumerable jokes and sketches about what our attitude to death says about our life: our morality and our manners, our honesty and hypocrisy, our vanity and our hubris (as Socrates remarked, 'To fear death, gentlemen, is no other than to think oneself wise when one is not, to think one knows what one does not know'). Each show had at least one sketch that said something about how we seek to make sense, and yet more often than not merely make nonsense, out of the end of all the days: there was the one where the mourners are all gathered round the coffin, and one of them remarks, 'He was a terrible man – he always seemed to have the last word'– at which point the coffin lid slides open and an angry voice bellows out from inside: 'No, I didn't!'; there was another one about the priest at a funeral who says, 'Please accept this last soul into Heaven,' only to be startled when the Devil pops up and says, 'I'm sorry, but this one belongs to me!'; then there was the one about the harassed-looking little man who barges through the mourners and crashes into the coffin ('I always said he'd be late for his own funeral,' mutters his long-suffering wife); and another about Richard the Lionheart, sitting down on a barren English hillside, slipping into a deep depression just as, unbeknown to him, the Grim Reaper is creeping up behind him ('Shall I end it all now,' he asks himself, 'with one quick stroke of my sword and find eternal peace? Yes, that is what I shall do!' He then pulls back his sword and, in doing so, hits the Grim Reaper hard in the groin). One of Dave Allen's own personal favourites concerned the death of an old actor: 'Imagine the scene: he is being cremated, and there is the coffin and the small curtain area behind it, and the old clergyman pays tribute to this knight of the theatre who has brought the Bard to the stage, providing pleasure and enjoyment . . . and he is rambling on, then he says, "In terms of the theatrical profession he is about to take his last final call." With that, the curtains open and the coffin disappears behind the aperture and the curtains close. And the congregation starts to applaud. Suddenly, the curtains open again and the coffin comes out and takes another call.'

'The clergy themselves have great humour, there's no doubt about that,' said Allen. 'It's the interpretation of what people get [from worshipping God] that's puzzling. I was doing a sketch in a graveyard – I like graveyards, they are good places for laughs – the idea being about the man *who invented down payment on hire purchase coffins. This man hadn't finished paying before he died, so he only got half a coffin. So we are walking up the road towards the graveyard and we are all in black, beautifully dressed, and we have mourners – we're an authentic kosher funeral – and coming down towards us is another funeral – a real funeral – and we have this coffin with a pair of legs sticking out the back and we both divide and we split, and the faces on these people – these legs are actually wobbling. Now the vicar of their lot comes up to me afterwards, and he is the personification of an English curate: he has the most enormous Adam's apple, and the dog collar is about five sizes too big, and dandruff like snow storms. And he says in a funny voice: "I do enjoy your shows very much, but you do tend – how can I put it? – to portray us clergy-men as stupid arseholes."'*

There were so many 'death-related' sketches during the run of Dave Allen At Large that, even now, many who grew up watching them will instinctively describe anything odd or eccentric or embarrassing that they witness at a funeral as one more 'Dave Allen moment'. What links them all together is the fact that, in spite of any context of sadness, they make us smile.

G.M.

Death in Life

Wakes

A very important part of the Irish way of life is death. You see, if anybody else, anywhere else in the world, dies, that's the end of it – they're dead. But in Ireland, when somebody dies we lay them out and watch them for a couple of days. It's called a 'wake', and it's a party, it's a send-off. The fella is laid out on the table and there's drinking and dancing and all the food you can eat. And all your friends come from all over the place and they all stand around the wake table looking at you with a glass in their hands and they say, 'Here's to yer health!' The terrible thing about dying over there is that you miss your own wake! It's the best day of your life. You've paid for everything and you can't join in! Mind you – if you did, you'd be drinking on your own.

There are so many stories, so many gags, so many jokes about the wake. There's the one, for example, about the hospitality of the host who was the deceased: the rule was that you couldn't partake in the hospitality at all unless you could actually say something very good about the man. And there was this wake in Northern Ireland where they're all standing around this man who's the most detested man in the town, and all the booze is there – a gallon of whiskies, gins and brandies, ports and sherries – and nobody can think of a nice thing to say about this man, so nobody can have a drink. And the barber eventually says: 'Well . . . he wasn't a hard man to shave.'

Shedding Skin

Do you know that we all shed skin? Do you know that each and every one of us, every man, woman and child in the world, sheds skin? Over an hour, each and every one of us sheds something like ten thousand minute scales of skin. Over a three-day period, we shed one total layer of skin. This is fact; it's not made-up, it's fact. Do you know that something like ninety per cent of the dust in the world is made up from dead human skin? How do you feel about that? You think you're dusting your house – you're not. You're just moving your grandmother around.

~

Fear of Death

A man – a great drinker – is in the pub one night. And it's what we call in Ireland 'a nasty night': a storm, dark clouds, thunder, lightning. And he's in the pub and he's thinking to himself: 'God, that's a terrible night! That's a night for all the banshees! That's a night for all of them black and tans to be walkin' about! I'm not walkin' home the long way tonight! I'll take the shortcut through the graveyard!' Now, unknown to him, a new grave has been dug in the graveyard for the morrow. So he leaves the bar, and, as he weaves his merry way around the grave stones, he comes to this empty grave which he doesn't see. *Phuum!* He's into it. And with the mud, the rain and the slime, every time that he climbs up and gets to the edge of the opening of the grave, he slides slowly back in again. And so he thinks to himself: 'I'll stay the night.'

And half-an-hour later, another fella leaves the same pub and decides to take the same shortcut home through the graveyard. He weaves his merry way around the grave stones, comes to the same grave and *phuum!* – he's into it. Like the first one, every time that he tries to get out of it, he slides slowly back in again.

The first one is sitting there looking at him. He stands up, taps the other fella on the shoulder and says: 'You'll never get out!'

He did.

~

Before They Go

The 98-year-old Mother Superior from Poland was dying. The nuns gathered around her bed trying to make her last journey comfortable. They gave her some warm milk to drink but she refused. Then one of the nuns took the glass back to the kitchen. Remembering a bottle of Irish whiskey received as a gift the previous Christmas, she opened it and poured a generous amount into the warm milk. Back at Mother Superior's bed, she held the glass to her lips. Mother drank a little, then a little more and, before they knew it, she had the whole glass down to the last drop. 'Mother,' the nuns asked with earnest, 'please give us some wisdom before you die.' She raised herself up in bed and, with a pious look on her face, said: 'Don't sell that cow.'

＊

A man comes out of a cave following a period of seclusion and contemplation, and discovers that, in his absence, the surface of the world has been destroyed. All the cities have been levelled, and there's not a living human being to be found anywhere. He travels across the country, searches all over the place, and doesn't find a single person. He travels all around the world – the Near East, the Far East, across the ocean to America. It is the same everywhere. The trip has taken him eight years, and he has still not found a single individual. Finally, he comes to the top of the Empire State Building. He looks down, stares at all the emptiness, and thinks that there is no way that he can stand to live all by himself. He simply could not stand to go on living without other people. So he decides that he will jump off and destroy himself. On the way down, however, he hears a phone ringing . . .

＊

There is a custom in Ireland that a dying man is allowed one question before he dies which must be answered completely truthfully otherwise the soul is damned. And you get a little fella dying. He's got four sons: three of the biggest fellas you've ever seen in your life and one skinny little puny *nothin'*. So he's lying there on his deathbed and he tells his wife: 'Mary, are you there, darlin'? Are you there?' She goes: 'I'm here, love. I'm here beside you.' He says: 'I'm goin'. I'm goin' now.' She says: 'I know. Don't hang about now.' So he looks up and says: 'Mary, before I go, I'm going to ask you The Question. Tell me now, is that skinny little runt standing at the end of the bed, is he *really* my son?' She says: 'He is. Honest to God. He *is* your son.' And he goes: 'Uhhhh . . .' She looks up and says, 'Thank God he didn't ask about the other three!'

*

There was a very old man who had spent his entire life acquiring his fortune. Finally, he was dying in bed at home as the doctor and the priest came to pay him a visit. The doctor asks him: 'Sir, before you go, could you pay me £15,000 for all of the medical bills and expenses?' The priest adds: 'And, I'm afraid, sir, I'll need another £15,000 for the funeral, burial and services.' 'Very well,' the old man answers, 'but when you bury me, tell my wife that I went just like our Lord.' The doctor and the priest respond in the same way: 'How do you mean, sir?' The old man replies: 'Between two thieves.'

*

There's one of those old saloons in the Wild West. Like in the movies. The piano is tinkling away, some old-timers are hunched over a table playing cards, one or two cowboys are standing by the bar smoking and drinking. And suddenly, the doors swing open and a stranger comes in. A tall man, with a black hat, a black moustache, a black bow-tie and a black tailcoat. 'Hey, boy!' he shouts out in the direction of one of the regulars. 'I wanna talk to yer!' The piano stops playing. The chattering comes to an abrupt halt. The old-timers are holding their cards in mid-air, as if frozen. Everybody is looking up and waiting for something to happen. The place is now absolutely silent. The regular there turns around, walks over towards this man, fixes him with an aggressive stare and says: 'Stranger, in this town we shoot first and ask questions afterward!' The stranger pulls out his gun and shoots – *Bang! Bang! Bang!* – killing the other man dead. Then he says: 'Could you tell me where the railway station is?'

*

A priest says to the man on his deathbed: 'My son, do you renounce the Devil and all his teachings?' The dying man replies: 'With all due respect, Father, this is really not the time to be making enemies!'

~

After They've Gone

When I was a young boy back in Ireland, I always used to think that the words spoken by the priest at a funeral were: 'In the name of the Father, the Son and into the hole he goes.' It made sense to me at the time. I suppose, in a way, it still does.

*

It's a very healthy country, Ireland. A *very* healthy country. As a matter of fact, all graveyards hire fellas to walk around with big sticks going: 'Get back in the hole!'

*

When a person dies in Ireland, there's not a lot of crying. What they do is have a wake: it's a party that doesn't celebrate that they're gone, but that they're going on to a better place. One time, a couple of fellas look at the body in the coffin: 'We're going to have to do something,' says one of them. 'H-He's getting in the way of the dancing.' The other one says: 'Well, we-we can't get rid of him – he's the host!' So the first fella says: 'I've got an idea. He's warm, he'll bend – we'll stick him in a chair and get rid of the coffin!' The other one says: 'Now, now, that's what I call thinking, boy! You-You've got a bit of the old grey matter up there! With brains like that, you-you should be a bus conductor!' So they pull the body out of the coffin, and are fussing with him to find him a seat. They yell out: 'S-Somebody give us a chair for Murphy!' An old drunk at the back of the room yells back: 'Hip-hip-hooray!'

*

I live near a graveyard which actually has a sign that says: 'Do not use the footpath to the crematorium – it is for patrons only.'

*

Mary Clancy goes up to Father O'Grady after his Sunday morning sermon. She's in tears. He says, 'So what's bothering you, Mary, my dear?' She says, 'Oh, Father, I've got terrible news. My husband passed away last night.' The priest says, 'Oh, Mary, that's terrible. Tell me, my dear, did he happen to have any last requests?' She says, 'That he did, Father.' The priest says, 'What did he ask, Mary?' She says, 'He said, "Please, Mary, put down that damn gun . . ."'

*

A man is visiting a graveyard, and he comes across another man there, crying at a gravestone, screaming: '*Why?* Why did you *die?*' The onlooker asks: 'Was this your mother?' The sobbing man keeps crying and squeals: 'Go away!' The other man asks: 'Was it your brother?' In between sobs, the man again squeals: '*No!*' The other man asks: 'Could it have been your sister?' The grieving man screams: '*NO!*' and resumes sobbing and crying: '*WHY DID YOU DIE?*' The questioner asks, 'A friend?' The sobbing man looks up and cries: '*It was my wife's first husband!*'

*

The Irish are supposed to be what we call a 'demonstrative' nation. But the Italians are even worse. There's an Italian. His wife has died. And all the way out to the graveyard, he's going: 'Aghh! *[Sobs]* What am I gonna do? Aagh! Why-a-why? What am I gonna do?' Then they stick the coffin in, and he goes: 'Waaaaghh!' And all the way back in the car he's going: '*Wee-aagh-ha-aaagh!* What am I gonna *do?*' And his friend says: 'Mario! You must-a pull yourself together! I know you loved her. I *know* you loved her! But she is a dead. You must-a live-a your life! In six months' time you will meet *another* beautiful girl. And you will fall in love. And you will marry.' He says: '*Six months? What am I gonna do TONIGHT?*'

*

This character is touring through a very rural part of Ireland. Normally, all of the towns there that he comes to are very open and very friendly, they'll say, 'Come in, have some bacon, some eggs, have a jar,' they're very warm and welcoming. But he gets to this one town where there's not a sound. There's total quiet, and a real stillness about the place. All the shutters are pulled down, all the doors are locked, and, as he walks through the empty streets, all that he sees is the odd curtain of a house move slightly, revealing a little face or two, staring at him, as he passes by. He eventually comes to the town square, and there in the square is a funeral entourage. And behind the coffin is a gigantic man, a huge man dressed in black, with a face that looks like it's been cut from granite – a shock of hard grey hair, a pair of ice-cold eyes and a great sharp chin – and held on a lead in his left hand is an enormous Irish wolfhound. A great big dark dog, a fierce-looking dog, double the size of a normal Irish wolfhound, with a huge tongue lolling out and eyes the colour of blood. And behind the man and this dog is another man dressed in black, and behind that man is another man, and behind him is another man – there's thirty-nine of them altogether, dressed in black, walking behind this coffin. There's not a woman anywhere. Just these men. And the fella thinks: 'That's an incredible funeral. I've never seen a funeral like that before.' He's totally enthralled, and, as he can't contain his curiosity, he goes up to this great big granite-faced man at the front and he says: 'Excuse me, but what's happening here? Has somebody very *important* died?' The big fella says: 'No. Not really.' So the stranger asks: 'Who is it? Who has died?' He says: 'Me wife. I'm burying me wife.' The stranger says: 'Oh, really? Then obviously, judging by the atmosphere of this funeral, she must have been a deeply loved person.' The big man says: 'No. She was not. She was the most despised person in the whole of this town. Everybody hated her. Everybody prayed every day that she'd die. But she didn't.' And the stranger says: 'Nobody liked her at all?' 'Nope,' said the man. 'Nobody liked her, nobody loved her. She was a despised person.' So the stranger says: 'Well, that dog – is that her dog? Obviously *he* must have loved her very much for you to have brought him to her funeral.' The man says: 'No. The dog hated her. The dog killed her. This is the dog that savaged her. Bit her throat out that dog did.' And the stranger says: 'Really?' He thinks for a moment and then he says: 'Um . . . could I possibly *buy* that dog?' And the big fella says: 'Get to the end of the queue.'

*

There was this old farmer, in Ireland, who was ploughing up his field one day when he ploughed up an old cemetery on his property. So he got it into his mind to sell some of the skulls to the tourists at the nearby airport. 'Excuse me, sir,' he said to one of them. 'Are you, by any chance, an American?' The visitor replied: 'Yes, I'm an American.' So the farmer asks him: 'How would you like a very special souvenir of old Ireland?' He looks around nervously. 'The skull of Brian Boru – the greatest king of all Ireland! Would you like to buy that?' The American is intrigued: 'Are you trying to tell me that *this* is actually the skull of a legitimate Irish king?' 'I am, that, yes,' says the farmer. So the American asks: 'How much do you want for it?' 'Well,' the farmer looks around nervously. 'It's been in my family for generations, but I suppose I can sell it to you for, er, a couple of quid.' So he sells him the skull. A few months later, the farmer meets the same American at the same airport, but the farmer has been drinking and doesn't recognise him. 'Excuse me, sir, would you happen to be an American?' The visitor says: 'Yes, I am.' The farmer says: 'Then how would you like to buy the skull of none other than Brian Boru?' The American is taken aback: 'What are you talking about? You already sold me the skull of Brian Boru a few months ago – and *that* one's smaller than the one you already sold me!' So the farmer goes: 'Oh, yes, well, you see, this is when he was a boy . . .'

*

You can tell a lot about the history and character of a town or a village or wherever just by wandering through a graveyard. It's fascinating. The only thing that puzzles me is that there are all these eulogies for people: the husband who was a brilliant father and a lovely man who's deeply missed, and the wife who was the sweetest woman that ever walked on this earth. There are all of these wonderful things telling you about how wonderful all of these people were, and every time I look at them I think: where are all the bad bastards buried?

*

I had this friend of mine whose wife died, and he buried her, and then he got married again. And after about fifteen years of marriage, the second wife died. So the priest said: 'Well, where do you want to bury her?' And the man said: 'I want her to be buried beside my first wife'. And the priest said: 'Where, when *you* die, do you want to be buried?' He said: 'Well, bury me between them both . . . but would you lean me towards Aggie?'

8

The Afterlife

Laying my bulbs in the dark,
Visions have I of hereafter.
Lip to lip, breast to breast, hark!
No more weeping, but laughter!

Katharine Tynan

~

*D*ave Allen always respected those who felt the need, personally and privately, to believe in an afterlife. He could see how loss could compel them to make such a leap of faith, because he still felt, quite acutely, the loss of, among others, his father, Cullie. 'I do miss him,' he told one interviewer. 'And I have extraordinary dreams, too, about my father. Where I find him. And he is now younger than I am. And I always ask him why he went away, why did he go away, and he always has some sort of reason that he had to go – he couldn't tell anyone but he had to go. It's a recurring dream.'

It remained, however, only a dream for him. He really was an atheist – or at least, as Brendan Behan put it, a 'daylight atheist' – and his outlook stayed honest and earthbound. 'I don't believe in Heaven,' he told one interviewer. 'I think Heaven is where you want it to be. And I don't believe in having a conversation with somebody who isn't there.' When asked why he always ended his shows by saying, 'May your God go with you,' he explained: 'The reason for that is that there are so many gods – you know, there are Muslim gods and Jewish gods and Christian gods and Buddhist gods and Hindu gods – and we're a multi-national society now, so "may your God go with you," whichever it is that you choose. "May he go with you" – that's all.'

He began one show in the 1980s with a sketch that saw a white-haired and white-bearded God being shaken from his slumbers by a Catholic priest, who calls out: 'Oh Lord, I beseech thee in my hour of need as a minister of the one and only true faith, to answer these my prayers. Oh Lord, your Church lives in troubled times . . .' At this point another voice, this one belonging to a Muslim priest, calls out: 'In the name of Allah the Beneficent, the Merciful, praise be . . .' Then a third voice, this one belonging to a rabbi, joins in, followed soon after by that of an Anglican, and then a Buddhist, and so on and so on, each one of them adding to the babble of spiritual presumptuousness, until God can take it no more: 'Ah, shut up!' He cries. 'God in Heaven help me!' At this point, the voice of the Prime Minister of the time, Margaret Thatcher, breaks through: 'Yes?'

This is what Dave Allen mocked – not the private beliefs, but the public pomposity of those who worked so assiduously to sustain the scriptural soap opera about Him Upstairs and Him Downstairs, the otherworldly equivalents of Popeye and Bluto. The critics applauded him for both his audacity and his humanity ('He's a blaspheming atheist on the side of the angels,' wrote Charles Spencer) and, in spite of the best efforts of the tabloid troublemakers, most religious people got the joke. An Australian magazine celebrated the start of a new Dave Allen tour with the headline: 'OUR FATHER, WHO ART IN HEAVEN, WON'T LET DAVE GO TO HELL', and, when he returned to his homeland to play Dublin's Gaiety Theatre, someone saw him backstage after his first night performance and said, 'They're saying you're God's own comedian.' He gave a shy little smile as he raised a glass of champagne close to his lips: 'Dammit,' he said. 'I like that . . .'

G.M.

~

Fire and Brimstone

You get in Ireland what we call the 'fire and brimstone' preachers. You get the fella in the pub and he's saying: '*I WILL TELL YOU! I WILL TELL YOU ABOUT THE GREAT JUDGEMENT DAY! I WILL TELL YOU ON THAT DAY THE GREAT BOOK WILL BE OPENED! AND ALL YOUR SINS – WHETHER MENTAL OR PHYSICAL – WILL BE IN THAT BOOK! AND THE LORD WILL BANISH THE WICKED! AND THERE WILL BE A GREAT WEEPING AND A GNASHING OF TEETH!* There's an old woman down the front and she says: 'I don't have any teeth.' And he says: '*TEETH WILL BE PROVIDED!*'

~

Purgatory

When people talk about the afterlife, they always talk about Heaven and Hell. They never talk about Purgatory. Purgatory is the place in between – it's a place where the people who are not very good and not very bad are sent for a period while it's being decided whether to send them up to Heaven or down to Hell. And there were these two fellas in Purgatory who agreed to keep in touch after they'd been moved on. Eventually, one of them went to Heaven and one of them went to Hell. So the fella in Heaven rings the fella in Hell and asks: 'What's it like down there?' The fella in Hell says: 'It's very good, actually. It's not as bad as I thought it was going to be. There are a lot of old friends here. A couple of hours each day we've got to stoke some coal into the furnaces, and that's all. What's it like up there in Heaven?' The other fella says: 'Very hard. I've got to get up at four o'clock in the morning and go out and pull in all the stars, and roll up the night, and pick up the moon and bring it in, and take out the sun and roll out all the clouds. And then, at about five o'clock in the evening, I've got to go back out and take the sun in, and roll up all the clouds again, and bring out the stars and stick the moon out again.' The other fella says: 'That sounds like hard work!' 'It is!' moans his friend: 'It's twenty-three hours a day!' So the fella in Hell says: 'Well, *why* are you working that hard?' The fella in Heaven replies: 'Well, there's only two of us up here!'

~

Heaven

God must be insane to make an invisible place and then put a wall and a gate around it!

~

Hell

There's a rabbi, a Catholic priest and an Anglican vicar descending through the stages of Hell. At the first stage, the priest gets out and it's all flames and arid desert. Then they go down to the next stage, and the rabbi gets out, and it's beautiful: trees, oranges, kibbutzes, everything. They go down one more level, and it's like the first one – flames and desert. The Anglican says to Satan: 'Why do we get *these*?' And Satan replies: 'Well, it's those Jewish people and their irrigation.'

*

When the Spanish dictator General Franco died, his Secretary of State tried to make contact with him by asking for help from God. 'He isn't here,' said God. 'He's in Hell.' So the Secretary of State sought out Satan, who said: 'Well, I'm afraid Franco's a bit busy at the moment.' This got the Secretary of State annoyed: 'Can't you pull him away from it? This is urgent!' Satan explained: 'Well, you see, he's making love to Cleopatra.' So the Secretary of State said: 'He's making love to Cleopatra? I thought Hell was punishment.' And Satan replied: 'It is for Cleopatra!'

~

Heaven and Hell

Many people think that Heaven and Hell are on different levels. They're not. They are side by side, separated by a fence. A wooden fence. One day, God was walking around the area and he started to inspect the fence. It was falling down. All bits and pieces had fallen off it. So he calls out to the Devil over the fence: 'Excuse, me. Mr Mephistopheles? *Hey, NICK!*' The Devil yells:

'Whaddyerwant?' God says: 'The fence. Look at it. It's falling down, it needs repairing. And the posts are on your side. This fence is your responsibility. When are you going to fix it?' The Devil says: 'Ah, screw you!' God says: 'Now, listen: if you do not do something about this fence very soon, you are going to hear from my solicitor!' The Devil says: 'Where are *YOU* going to find a solicitor?'

~

Outside the Pearly Gates

You know the Revd Ian Paisley? He'll die, he'll go to Heaven and knock on the Pearly Gates and say: 'I'd like to come in! I'd like to come in there and have a wee chat with yer man!' And St Peter looks at him and says: 'I've seen your face before.' Paisley says: 'I've been on television! I was on that *24 Hours* and *Panorama!*' St Peter says: 'Ah, yes, that's right – you're the, um, you're the Reverend Ian Paisley!' He says: 'I am! Can I come in?' St Peter says: 'Oh, no, I'm sorry, you're not in here. You're in the other place.' Paisley says: 'But I'm a man of God!' St Peter says: 'Yes, I know, the place is full of 'em – get off!' And off he goes. Two days later, there is another knock on the gates of Heaven. St Peter opens the gates. And standing there in his full regalia: Satan – Lucifer – the fallen angel – *Old Nick Himself!* With the *horns!* With the *tail! The fiery fork!* St Peter says: 'What do *you* want?' He says: 'I want political asylum from that fella down there!'

~

Inside the Pearly Gates

A man goes to Heaven, and St Peter shows him around. They go past one room, and the man asks: 'Who are all those people in there?' 'They are the Methodists,' says St Peter. They pass another room, and the man asks the same question. 'They are the Anglicans,' says St Peter. 'Hang on a minute,' says the man, 'do you mean everyone gets in here?' St Peter replies: 'Well, as long as they've led decent lives.' So on they go. As they're approaching the next room, St Peter whispers: 'Take your shoes off and tiptoe by as quietly as you can.' 'Why, who's in there?' asks the man. 'The Catholics,' says St Peter, 'and they think that they're the only ones up here.'

*

There was a man in Ireland, he was seventy-seven years old and had worked eighty hours a week all his life and never had a holiday. His children were all married and his wife had died. So he decided to enjoy life. He had a face-lift, he got an expensive new toupee, he bought ten new suits and a brand new car. One evening, he got all dressed up in a smart new suit and a smart new tie, put on his new toupee, got into his new car and drove off towards Dublin. He had only gone a mile when he was killed in an accident. On arrival in Heaven, he walks over to St Peter and says, 'What's going on here? All my life I worked hard, and finally, when I finally had everything in place to start enjoying myself, I was killed. *Why?* Why did you let it happen?' St Peter bows his head in embarrassment and says, 'Well, to tell you the truth, I didn't recognise you.'

~

Most Haunted: Almost Live

You get a ventriloquist who's not a very successful ventriloquist, and he hears about mediums contacting the people in the afterlife, and he thinks: 'That's not a bad job. I can throw my voice. I could make a fortune as a medium!' So he opens up. And the first customer walks in and she says: 'I would like to hear my husband speak from the Beyond. And if I can hear my husband speak, I shall give you £100.' And he says: 'Madam, for £100, not only will you hear your husband speak, but you will hear him speak as I drink a glass of water!'

~

A Cold Call

The Vatican. The Pope's secretary comes running into the office and says: 'Your Holiness! It's Him! *Him!* He's come back! He's riding up the street on a donkey, and all the people are waving palm leaves at him and shouting "Hosannah!" and he's headed this way!' At which the Pope begins shuffling papers around on his desk and says: 'Look busy!'

~

Meeting Your Maker

What would I say to God? Well, the first thing I'd say is: 'Good afternoon, madam!'

*

Why do we always assume that God is a man? Maybe God is a woman. Maybe God is black. Maybe God is a black woman. Maybe He's dead. Maybe He's a dead black woman.

*

They say to me that if I'm good I'll go to Heaven, and if I'm wicked in life I'll go to Hell. Then I think: I've wandered through life, and I've met an awful lot of what I would call 'godly' good people, and they were goody-goodies, kind of *creepy* goody – I mean, they're thinking 'me' all the time: '*I* love God, *I* go to church all the time, *I* pray ...' – all of that – so that means that Heaven's going to be full of that lot. Can you imagine being stuck with that lot for eternity? Hell, on the other hand, is going to be full of the most interesting people. So I'll be happy to go to Hell. But then God, I suppose, would know that Hell would not be Hell for me. It would be Heaven. So he won't send me to Hell. He'll send me to Heaven.

Before You Go

~

We were in a bar and had had a couple of drinks, and somebody started to talk about the unknown, the spirit world, and the conversation came up about the gravedigger's house, and the locals started to tell us about it. This gravedigger was found in his bed, dead, with terrible marks upon his neck and his eyes wide open. And the doctors said that the marks had had nothing to do with his death, but that the man had died of fright. And I scoffed. Foolishly. And it came about, with a few more drinks and everything else, that I accepted a dare, or a bet, that I would stay the night in the cottage beside the graveyard. And so I went there, and we agreed that the door would be locked, and I would stay in there until first light, and I was locked in. It was dank. It was cold. The effects of the booze began to wear off. And I began to think: 'What in the name of God are you doing?' And something – I don't know what it was, but it was something stronger than me – pulled me towards this bed where this man had died. And I was drawn – I fought against it but I was drawn – nearer and nearer to this bed. And I was told, somehow or other, to sit on that bed. I didn't want to, but I did. And an unnatural drowsiness came over me, and I became very sleepy, and I lay down – knowing full well that I shouldn't – and I went to sleep. A limbo sleep. And then I awoke – at what time I have no idea. The candle had burned down. It was black. It was cold. And I felt a presence. I was completely sober by this time and utterly terrified. I was paralysed by a presence of fear. And I felt something on my chest begin to move. It crept slowly up my chest. And I couldn't move. It came closer and closer to my throat. I gathered all my will-power, as this thing came closer, and closer, and I *grabbed* it, and it was wet and cold, and I *bit* it: *Aaaaaaggh!*

   . . . And that is how I lost my finger.[1]

*

1 Unless, that is, you find one of the following explanations more plausible: (a) 'Daddy and I were cutting wood. And, like all kids, I tended to find nostrils amazingly interesting. And I was picking my nose, and my father said: "If you continue to do that, I'll put your finger on the block and I'll chop your finger off!" So I stopped, but, after about three or four minutes, my finger found my nose again. And so he said: "All right: put your finger down there!" So I put my finger down there, and he raised the axe. He didn't think I'd keep my finger there, and I didn't think he'd bring the axe down . . .'; (b) 'I caught it in a cog when I was at school'; (c) 'It happened when I was a young boy. I was in church, and I laughed. The priest came

up to me and told me that if I ever laughed in church again, one of my fingers would fall off. I didn't believe him'; (d) 'I just lost it in the car door; somebody slammed the door shut and I didn't realise I'd left my hand there, so it just caught the tip of the finger when it shut'; (e) 'It was bitten off by a dog. I saw this great big grey-haired dog, a very handsome-looking Irish wolfhound, and I asked the man who was standing by it, "Does your dog bite?" and he said, "Ah, no, good as gold, he is, my dog, a real old softie," so I went to stroke the dog and it got me. I said to the man, "I thought you said your dog doesn't bite?" The man said, "Well, *he* doesn't. As for this dog here, though, I'd advise a measure of caution"'; (f) 'What happened to my finger? My arse ate it!'; (g) 'No mystery: I was in a car accident. Nine-and-a-half fingers survived it'; (h) 'I was about nine years of age and – we used to eat in the kitchen – and I was sitting there, and I had something caught in my back tooth. And I was trying to pick it out with my finger, I was trying to get at this little bit of meat, and my brother John came in behind me, and he just saw me there – and we were always kind of at war continually, wrestling or something like that – and he just came in behind me and caught me like that *[pulls an arm up hard under his jaw]* and my jaw closed, and I bit my finger right through. I went 'Aagaagh' and took the finger out. And that was it.' (As the man himself always said: 'A good storyteller never lets the facts get in the way of the tale.')

TV & Film Credits

TELEVISION

A: Series & Specials

Tonight with Dave Allen (Australia: Channel 9)
1963–1964

The Val Doonican Show (BBC1)

Series One:
07.10.1965 – 16.12.1965 (11 episodes)
Series Two:
22.10.1966 – 14.01.1967 (4 episodes)

Producer/Director: John Ammonds

Around with Allen (ABC/ITV)

Special:
05.03.1967

Script: Eric Merriman
Producer/Director: Malcolm Morris

Tonight with Dave Allen (ATV/ITV)

Series One:
09.07.1967 – 01.10.1967 (13 episodes)
Special:
23 December 1967
Series Two:
29.09.1968 – 19.01.1969 (17 episodes)

Script: Dave Allen
Additional material: Eric Merriman (Series One and
Special),
George Martin (Series Two)
Directors: Gordon Reece (Series One),
Colin Clews and Anthony Flanagan (Special)
Colin Clews and David Foster (Series Two)
Producers: Gordon Reece (Series One)
Colin Clews (Special and Series Two)

The Dave Allen Show (BBC2)

Special:
23.06.1968
Special:
08.06.1969

Script: Dave Allen, Ian Davidson,
Additional material: Bill Stark/Bernie Sharp, Brad
Ashton, Michael Bentine, David Cumming, Eric
Merriman
Producer/Director: Ernest Maxin

The Dave Allen Show (BBC1)

11.10.1969 – 01.11.1969 (3 episodes)

Script: Dave Allen, Ian Davidson,
Additional material: Bill Stark/Bernie Sharp,
Brad Ashton, Michael Bentine, David Cumming, Eric
Merriman
Producer/Director: Ernest Maxin

Dave Allen in the Melting Pot (ITV)

Special:
23.12.1969

Script: Dave Allen
Director: Bob Heller
Producer: Bob Heller

Dave Allen (Australia: Seven Network)

Special:
02.05.1970

Script: Dave Allen
Director: Anon

Inside the Mind of Dave Allen (Thames/ITV)

Special:
08.07.1970

Script: Dave Allen, Bill Stark, Chris Hughes
Producer/Director: John Robins

The Dave Allen Show (Australia: Nine Network)

Special:
18.09.1971
(with Peter Cook and Dudley Moore)

Script: Dave Allen
Director: John Collins

Dave Allen At Large (BBC2)

Series One:
21.01.1971 – 01.04.1971 (6 episodes)
Series Two:
27.01.1972 – 06.04.1972 (6 episodes)
Series Three:
15.01.1973 – 26.03.1973 (6 episodes)
Special:
21.01.1974
Series Four:
27.02.1975 – 03.04.1975 (6 episodes)
Series Five:
18.10.1976 – 20.12.1976 (6 episodes)

Special:
24.04.1978
Special:
26.12.1979 (BBC1)

Script: Dave Allen, Peter Vincent, Austin Steele
Additional material: Ian Davidson
Producer/Director: Peter Whitmore

Dave Allen in Search of the Great English Eccentric
(ATV/ITV)

Special:
08.10.1974

Script: Dave Allen
Producer/Director: Robin Brown
Producer: Bob Heller

The Dave Allen Show (Australia: Seven Network)

Series:
1975 (4 episodes)

Script: Dave Allen
Director: Kevin Burston

The Dave Allen Show (Australia: Nine Network)

Series:
1977 (6 episodes)

Script: Dave Allen
Director: Kevin Burston

Dave Allen and Friends (ATV/ITV)

04.01.1977 – 29.03.1977 (12 episodes)

Script: Dave Allen
Producer/Director: Robin Brown

The Dave Allen Special (Australia: Nine Network)

13.03.1979

Script: Dave Allen

Dave Allen Presents Unusual Oddities
(Australia: ATN 7)

19.04.1979

Script: Dave Allen
Producer/Director: Robin Brown

Dave Allen (BBC1)

Special:
20.04.1981
Special:
29.05.1981 (BBC2)
Special:
26.12.1984

Special:
08.04.1985
Special:
31.12.1986
Series:
06.01.1990 – 10.02.1990 (6 episodes)

Script: Dave Allen, Peter Vincent, Ian Davidson,
Paul Alexander
Additional material: Penny Hallowes, Dick Vosburgh,
Andrew Marshall/David Renwick/Barry Cryer
Andy Hamilton, Dick Fiddy/Mark Wallington
Director: Bill Wilson
Producers: Bill Wilson (6 episodes)
Bill Wilson and Peter Whitmore (3 episodes)
James Moir (2 episodes)

Dave Allen (Carlton/ITV)

Series:
07.01.1993 – 18.02.1993 (7 episodes)
Special:
26.12.1994

Script: Dave Allen, Ian Davidson, Peter Vincent
Additional material: Kevin Day, Chips Hardy, Nick
Revell, Penny Hallowes
Script editors: Ian Davidson, Peter Vincent
Director: Tom Poole
Producer: Nick Symons

The Unique Dave Allen (BBC1)

31.12.1997 – 01.02.1998 (6 episodes)
Director: Dave Morley

B: One-Off Appearances

New Faces (BBC TV)

1959

The Blackpool Show (ABC/ITV)

24.07.1964

Sunday Night at the London Palladium (ATV/ITV)

10.01.1965

The Toast of the Town (US:CBS)

19.03.1967

The Big Show (ATV/ITV)

21.04.1968

Royal Television Gala Performance (BBC1)

24.05.1970

Parkinson (BBC1)

21.09.1974

TV & Film Credits

One Fine Day (LWT/ITV)

17.02.1979

Cast: Dave Allen (Phillips); Robert Stephens (Welby);
Dominic Guard (Rycroft); Barbara Leigh-Hunt (Mrs
Phillips); Leslie Sands (Commissionaire)

Script: Alan Bennett
Producer/Director: Stephen Frears

Parkinson (BBC1)

31.10.1981

Aspel & Company (LWT/ITV)

03.09.1988

Aspel & Company (LWT/ITV)

12.01.1991

The Clive James Show (BBC1)

03.03.1991

Des O'Connor Tonight (Thames/ITV)

11.12.1996

Clive Anderson All Talk (BBC1)

12.11.1998

Stand Up with Alan Davies (BBC1)

19.06.2000

MOVIES

Squeeze a Flower (1970)

Cast: Jack Albertson (Alfredo Brazzi), Walter Chiari (Brother George), Rowena Wallace (June Phillips), Kirrily Nolan (Maria), Dave Allen (Tim O'Mahony), Alec Kellaway (The Abbot), Michael Laurence (Brother James), Alan Tobin (Brother Peter), Charles McCallum (Brother Sebastian), Harry Lawrence (Vequis), Roger Ward (Bosun), Sandy Harbutt (Grape Picker), Jeff Ashby (Bert Andrews), Penny Sugg (Stewardess), Sue Lloyd (The Receptionist), Barry Crocker (Waiter), Lyndal Moore (Lab Assistant), Beryl Cheers (Housewife), Bobby Limb (Bobby Lambert), Dawn Lake (Dawn Lambert), Amanda Irving (Worker), Franz Zach (Italian Father), Alex Mozart (Truck Driver), Lea Densfield (Flower Seller), Olga Yarad (Maid)

Script: Charles Isaacs
Cinematography: Brian West
Editor: Stanley Moore
Director: Marc Daniels

VIDEOS & DVDs

VHS:

Dave Allen (1994)

BBC Worldwide BBCV 5374

Vintage Dave Allen (1996)

PolyGram Video PolyGram 6399203

Dave Allen: Back to Back (2000)

Universal B00004YA494

DVD:

Dave Allen ... On Life (2005)

Universal DVD 823 092 9 11

The Best of Dave Allen (2005)

BBC Region 2 DVD CCD30186

Notes

~

1 Brian O'Nolan (1911–1966) was a member of the Irish Civil Service who, under his various pseudonyms (civil servants were not permitted to publish under their real names), wrote some of the most distinctive prose of his time. As Myles na Gopaleen, he contributed a brilliantly sharp and inventive satirical column in the *Irish Times* called 'Cruiskeen Lawn' (selections from which can now be found in a number of volumes, including *The Best of Myles* and *The Hair of the Dogma*). As Flann O'Brien, he was responsible for such novels as *At-Swim-Two-Birds* (1939), *The Third Policeman* (published posthumously in 1967) and *The Dalkey Archive* (1964).

2 See (or rather hear) the Dave Allen interview by Paul Jackson, *Talking Comedy*, BBC Radio 4, 6 April 2000.

3 See Gregory Castle, *Modernism and the Celtic Revival* (Cambridge: Cambridge University Press, 2001) and Philip O'Leary, *The Prose Literature of the Gaelic Revival, 1881–1921: Ideology and Innovation* (Pennsylvania: Penn State University Press, 1994).

4 Dave Allen, 'Introduction', *A Little Night Reading* (London: Roger Schlesinger, 1974), p. 15.

5 *Ibid.*

6 Dave Allen, *The Clive James interview*, BBC1, 3 March 1991. Allen also observed: '[C]onversation was very important: dinner conversation, conversations in bars, or striking up strange conversations with somebody at Lansdowne Road – then you're off into all sorts of rambling discourse, which needn't be hysterically funny, but can be interesting and amusing': quoted in 'How to get ahead in a hat', the *Observer*, Review section, 18 December 1994.

7 Dave Allen, interviewed by Paul Jackson, *Talking Comedy*, *op. cit.*

8 *Ibid.*

9 *Ibid.*

10 Dave Allen, quoted by Danielle Teutsch and Matthew Benns, 'Too rude for Oz TV', *Sun Herald* (Australia), 13 March 2005, p. 37.

11 Dave Allen, quoted by Sheridan Morley, 'Dave Allen: Reporter of Life', *The Times*, 12 January 1977, p. 9.

12 Dave Allen, interviewed by Paul Jackson, *Talking Comedy*, *op. cit.*

13 *Ibid.*

14 Dave Allen, interviewed by Clive Anderson, *Clive Anderson All Talk*, BBC1, 12 November 1998.

15 Dave Allen, undated written reminiscence, private family papers.

16 Dave Allen, interviewed by Paul Jackson, *Talking Comedy*, *op. cit.*

17 Dave Allen, *The Clive James interview*, *op. cit.*

18 Dave Allen, interviewed by Paul Jackson, *Talking Comedy*, *op. cit.*

19 Dave Allen, *The Clive James interview*, *op. cit.*

20 John Ammonds, interview with the editor, 12 July 2005.

21 *Ibid.*

22 Dave Allen, *Dave Allen Live*, programme notes, October 1986.

23 Dave Allen, quoted by Carol Sarler in the programme (produced by Proscenium Publications) accompanying his 1991 performances at the Strand Theatre in London.

24 *Squeeze a Flower* (1970), written by Charles Isaacs and directed by Marc Daniels.

25 'The Good Earth' (words and music by Ben Nisbet) / 'A Way of Life', released by Philips, BF 1748, in 1969. Dave Allen slightly altered the words as they were written – presumably to improve the scansion – when he came to record his spoken version.

26 Dave Allen, interviewed by Clive Anderson, *Clive Anderson All Talk, op. cit.*

27 Dave Allen, *The Clive James interview, op. cit.* (See 'Australians not amused', *The Times*, 14 September 1972, p. 7.)

28 Peter Whitmore, quoted by Jack Trevor-Story, 'Black humour in Lincoln green', *Radio Times*, 20 February 1975, p. 60.

29 Dave Allen, quoted by Gus Smith, *Dave Allen: God's Own Comedian* (London: Robert Hale, 1991), p. 187.

30 Ronnie Brody, *ibid.*

31 Michael Sharvell-Martin, interview with the editor, 12 August 2005. He recalled another memory of working with Allen: 'We were doing a sketch about David being carted off – quite literally – to an execution during the French Revolution, and we had hundreds of extras involved in the scene, and I was playing this strange hunchbacked character who was goading him. Well, David and I were getting very bored at one point, because filming was going on and on and on, and we'd already had about forty takes of this scene, so I just jumped up on the cart and whispered into David's ear: 'I suppose a fuck's out of the question?' And with that he collapsed and we had to do the scene yet again, but we couldn't help laughing, and we couldn't tell the director what exactly we were laughing at!'

32 Jacqui Clarke, interview with the editor, 14 August 2005.

33 Dave Allen, quoted in *The Sit-Down Stand-Up*, BBC Radio 4, 18 January 2005.

34 Peter Whitmore, *ibid.*

35 Richard Stone, *You Should Have Been In Last Night* (Sussex: The Book Guild, 2000), p. 99.

36 Bill Cotton, *Double Bill* (London: Fourth Estate, 2001), p. 153.

37 Dave Allen, quoted by Gus Smith, *op. cit.*, p. 80.

38 All of Dave Allen's notes are reproduced here with the permission of his family.

39 Hugh Stuckey, correspondence with the editor, 4 July 2005.

40 Dave Allen, speaking in 1998, quoted in the *Guardian*, 12 March 2005, p. 25.

41 Dave Allen, *The Clive James interview, op. cit.*

42 Dave Allen, interviewed by Clive Anderson, *Clive Anderson All Talk, op. cit.*

43 Jack Waterman, 'Taking the Mick', the *Listener,* 9 March 1978, pp. 301–2.

44 See the *Independent,* 17 February 1990, p. 16 and the *Daily Mirror,* 12 March 2005, p. 17.

45 Peter Vincent, quoted in *The Sit-Down Stand-Up*, BBC Radio 4, 18 January 2005. (The irony was that, as performed on the night, there was no 'fucking clock' on air, even though it was – and still is – misquoted in the media as having been present. The clock was fuck-free. The only 'fucking' was in the giving: 'And what do they fucking give you? A clock!' As, however, Dave Allen's intention had been to say 'fucking clock,' I have altered the transcript in Chapter 6 accordingly.)

46 The politician was Mr Robert Hayward, who was Conservative Member of Parliament at that time for the constituency of Kingswood. See *The Times,* 9 January 1990, p. 3; *The Sunday Times,* 14 January 1990, section C, p. 7; and *Parliamentary Debates (HANSARD)* (London: HMSO, 1990), Sixth Series, Volume 165, House of Commons, 16 January 1990, p. 173w.

47 Dave Allen, quoted by Gus Smith, *op. cit.*, p. 187.

48 Dave Allen, quoted in the *Daily Mirror,* 12 March 2005, p. 5.

49 See the following obituaries and appreciations: Stephen Dixon, 'Dave Allen: Irreverent comedian whose reflective monologues provoked outrage and delight', the *Guardian,* 12 March 2005, p. 25; Anthony Hayward, 'Dave Allen: Master of risqué stand-up comedy', the *Independent,* 12 March 2005, p. 45; anon, 'Dave Allen: Iconoclastic but essentially humane comedian who raged against the

absurdities of everyday life', *Daily Telegraph*, 12 March 2005, p. 29; Pete Clarke, 'An Appreciation', London *Evening Standard*, 12 March 2005, p. 9; Paul Clarke, 'A laugh divine', the *Stage*, 17 March 2005; and the tributes on the relevant pages of the BBC's website –<u>http://news.bbc .co.uk/1/hi/entertainment/tv and radio/ 4340909.stm</u> – and the comedy site Chortle – <u>http://www.chortle.co.uk/news/march05/ allen120301.php</u>.

A Note on the Contributors

~

Graham McCann is the acclaimed and best-selling author of *Frankie Howerd, Morecambe & Wise, Cary Grant* and *Dad's Army*.

*

Sir Bill Cotton, CBE, was Head of Light Entertainment at the BBC between 1970 and 1977, during which time he was responsible for overseeing the commissioning of a whole range of popular and iconic comedy programmes, including *Monthy Python's Flying Circus, The Two Ronnies, Morecambe & Wise* and a number of shows with Dave Allen. He was promoted to Controller of BBC 1 in 1977 and then, in 1981, to Managing Director of Television at the BBC, a role he fulfilled until his retirement in 1987.

He has been awarded the CBE and received a knighthood for his services to British Broadcasting. He is Vice President of the Marie Curie Cancer Care charity.